THE SAXON
AND HER INFANT SAINT

Graham Wilton

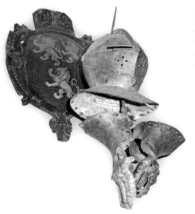

Cover: Stained glass detail from St Peter ad Vincula, South Newington

Frontispiece: Bloxham, St Mary, Thorneycroft Memorial

 First published in The Four Shires and Banbury Fare magazines in Great Britain 1997 - 2004 by Four Shires Publishing.
This compilation: The Saxon Princess and her Infant Saint published by Four Shires Publishing, Borough House, Marlborough Road, Banbury, Oxfordshire. OX16 5TH.
© Four Shires Publishing

A CIP catalogue record for this book is available from the British Library

ISBN 0 9548723 0 4

Photographs by Graham Wilton

Typeset in Palatino by Four Shires Publishing Ltd
Printed by Banbury Lithographic, Bloxham Mill,
        Oxfordshire

Contents

Introduction

I was just 13 when I first saw the multi-coloured statue of Sir John de Broughton in the church alongside the castle, and my imagination was fired by this trusty knight ready to do battle with the Saracens for his faith and the King.

As he lay there on top of his tomb with his sword by his side, I envisaged him, (fired by the stories by long forgotton authors like G.A.Henty, H.Rider Haggard, and Capt W.E.Johns) riding through the desert at the head of a band of trusty Oxfordshire men at arms following the banner of St George.

I was hooked. And from that moment onwards I have always visited any church, abbey or cathedral wherever I have been, because there are so many stories enshrined within the gorgeous buildings that are the repository of English history.

So if you read this book, as I hope you will, do not expect to find a learned treatise on church architecture, dogma, or dry as dust discourses on the virtues of one window arch compared to another, or you will be disappointed.

For this book contains a series of 28 articles written from a journalist and layman's point of view, with the accent on the people who worshipped, acted, sang, bartered and painted (often the most gory of pictures!) within the churches in the four or five counties in a 25 mile radius of an ancient market town, Banbury.

All the articles appeared in *The Four Shires*, or *Banbury Fare* magazines, and there are plenty of cross references to each of them. Because they were written over a period of five years, some of the details have been overtaken by time, and some of the context refers to what was happening then, but I think they are worth retelling.

I have often been asked which is my favourite among

the 60 or so churches which have been the subject of my articles. It is a very difficult question for even the smallest, or plainest of our treasury of churches has its own story to tell. But if I were pressed I would have to say St George's, Brailes, 'The Cathedral of the Feldons' for its commanding beauty, and Great Tew church for its sheer magic, which has little to do with its size.

For those of you who are interested in the technical aspect of the photographs of the churches, the majority were taken with 'steam' film cameras such as the Minolta Dynax 7, the Nikon F4, one or two on an Olympus 2n, and even a Zeiss Contarex. I did use a Bronica ETRs for at least one, and all the others were taken using a new fangled Olympus E20 digital camera. While it pains me (as a lifelong film man) to say it, I don't think anyone would be able to tell the difference between them.

My thanks go to George Walker of Bodicote whose wonderful drawings of churches in the Banbury area undoubtedly influenced me immensely: to my son Jeremy, who has put up with my demanding insistence to have the articles appear monthly in his *The Four Shires* and who has put the book together; to all those people who have written the potted histories of their own churches, and to the people I have encountered while photographing and writing, who have been either cleaning, preparing flowers or generally caring for these lovely buildings which are are dedicated to keeping English history alive for future generations to enjoy and marvel at.

The Saxon Princess and her Infant Saint

Legend has it that St Rumbold was born at Walton Fields a mile from King's Sutton's SS Peter and Paul church in AD 662. At his birth to a Saxon princess he declared: "I am a Christian" and he asked to be baptised by the name of Rumbold. He was duly baptised and a great stone was used as a font. He then died three days afterwards.

That font is now in the church, but it is only thanks to the Rev William Rennie, who was Vicar in 1921 that it is there at all.

On a glorious morning in February I was lucky enough to have a chat with Churchwarden Edward McGinlay, who has lived his entire life in King's Sutton, and among many other stories about his beloved church, he told me how the Vicar re-discovered the 1,300 year old font.

"In the 1920's a pinnacle fell from the tower into the churchyard luckily missing the church, but landing near a mound which we boys used to leapfrog over. When the Vicar arranged for the pinnacle to be moved he also asked for the mound to be removed as well because it was difficult to cut the grass around it. When it was dug into, the St Rumbold's font was found. We, of course, crossed the Vicar off our Christmas card list" chuckled Edward "because he had spoiled our favourite game".

The lead lined font was placed on a circular stone from Twyford Mill and remains in pride of place just inside the church door.

How had it become just a mound? It was down to the Victorians who had it removed and replaced. They were also responsible for removing the stone rood screen, and replacing it with the present wooden one after the design of Sir Giles Gilbert Scott, which is a feature of this church. It has been described as one of the famous churches of England, with its 198ft spire as one of the finest in a county of spires.

Most Banburyshire people will know the

rhyme: 'Adderbury for strength, Bloxham for length, and King's Sutton for beauty', and in King's Sutton's case it is certainly true for the spire and tower has a crown of thorns, splendid gargoyles, glorious pinnacles, delicate flying buttresses, symbols of the four Evangelists, finials, and numerous crockets.

It does present some perils however for as well as the pinnacle that fell into the churchyard, another one crashed through the church and lodged in the roof. The superb timberwork has been matched and replaced but the new work can just be identified.

Architect Brian Andrews who looks after the fabric of the church, although he is now retired, told me that a lightning conductor was placed on the steeple when some repair work was done, and within two years the spire was struck! It was fortuitous the conductor was there however for the damage was minimal.

"The churchwardens here are the most responsible people I have come across in our churches" he said " they really care for their church and do everything to ensure it is kept in good condition."

With a porch that was coming away from the church, and continual repairs needed, the support of both the congregation and the village is vital for this important and historic building.

Important because King's Sutton was the site of an ecclesiastical court when England had two forms of justice, one administered by the state, and the other by the church.

Surprisingly linked with Buckingham and Horley churches, the early Norman incumbents in 1276 were from the monastery at Peterborough, although there was certainly an earlier Saxon church which was rebuilt. It was part of the royal estates and was mentioned in the Domesday Book in 1086.

The current registers date from 1570 in the reign of Elizabeth I, and there is an ancient sundial on the parapet above the south aisle by the east end.

The north aisle which was built in 1320 has an altar dedicated to St Thomas of Canterbury, and it is possible that St Thomas a Becket prayed in the church on his way to Northampton Castle to meet King Henry II in the first week in October, 1164.

St Thomas was killed six years later.

The church has 40 numbered and several free (or reserved) pews with finials which are identical to those in Bodicote church.

The south porch has a door that is closed by a pulley and weight, the forerunner of a spring, and nearby is a Holy Water stoup, which Edward recalled was found by Mr Rennie in a farmyard in Mill Lane.

"He stopped to chat to some men who had been haymaking" said Edward "and noticed some chickens drinking from a stone bowl. He recognised it as one of two stoups and had both dug up and restored to the church."

The south aisle has an altar which was erected as a 1914-18 war memorial, and dedicated by Bishop Norman Lang in 1924. Near it are the stairs to the rood loft. The Chancel stands on Norman foundations and the arcading dates from 1100, although the present arches have been beautifully restored.

R.Rendell in a useful leaflet about the church mentions the works of the church clock which laboured manfully from 1696 to 1950.

"It had no face, the time being announced by the striking of a bell".

No visit to the church would be complete without mentioning St Rumbold's well, whose waters made the village famous as a fashionable spa from 1660 to 1777. Its fame came to an abrupt end in 1785 when a great fire destroyed 40 houses, and it is some measure of the wealth of the village of King's Sutton that £3287/16s/5d (a vast sum of money for the time) was collected for relief.

As a boy I used to cycle to Newbottle Woods, and passed the reputed outflow from the well in Astrop Park alongside the main Charlton road. While it fascinated us at the time no-one (probably wisely) was tempted to drink the rusty iron coloured liquid which trickled out!.

St Rumbold's mother insisted her husband (possibly the King of Northumbria) was baptised a Christian before she married him, and their son, as well as making his famous pronouncement added that he was soon to die, and wanted his body to remain at King's Sutton for a year, Brackley for two years and then to rest at Buckingham, where there was a shrine to him.

Still contemplating how an infant baby had the power of speech? George Walker of Bodicote in his finely illustrated book "Churches of the Banbury Area" which is still on sale and well worth a read, has a possible explanation: "Locally it is pointed out that the three days probably refer to his life after baptism."

So it is no great stretch of the imagination to believe that 'born' in this instance may well have been "born into the Christian church" possibly at puberty.

But as King's Sutton church has a touch of magic about it, I prefer to believe the tale of the Saxon princess and her baby that talked!

INTERESTED in England's glorious heritage in our churches? If so, head for Shenington where, with Alkerton just down the hill, you get two beautifully sturdy medieval buildings within easy walking distance.

If you drive, park alongside Shenington's spacious village green, and Holy Trinity's castellated tower emerges through the trees with an encitingly lovely view across the valleys towards Banbury.

young deer. Don't worry if you can't quite make it out, and it is difficult unless the light is right, for Harold Clifton in 1987, carved a superb replica in great detail, which has pride of place in the porch.

Harold (1915-1988) was the first Chairman of Cherwell District Council when it was formed from the Banbury Borough Council and Banbury RDC, and was a talented and likable man who set firm foundations for the new organisation.

The Rev Richard Hannah, who was Rector from 1963 suggests in his excellent booklet "Parishes and Churches 1989" which is illustrated by Pat Hannah, and well worth the minimal 50p, the man may have been a priest blessing the livestock, or that he was a farmer. Interestingly no other local church can

Shenington with Alkerton, once a Gloucestershire island in Oxfordshire

This is an early 12th century building but it was added to up to the 15th century, with a sizable 19th century restoration which saw one of its greatest treasures, the Norman arch moved to the side of the chancel to frame the organ pipes. It has typical zig zag and cable mouldings to delight the eye.

Before entering the church however, study the East wall where, despite the crumbling soft mellow golden Hornton stone can be seen a man in mediaeval tunic under an ornate arch and beside him is an ox, or as I suspect, the representation of a

boast a similar figure in the multitude of carvings which abound.

Jump forward 500 years and dominating the south wall inside the church is the scarlet and gold banner of the Shenington Amicable Society dated 1841 to 1891.

Formed in 1841 it was limited to 121 members who each subscribed three shillings (15p) each quarter, and there was an annual church service and dinner on Trinity Tuesday attended by musicians who were paid up to two guineas

(£ 2.10p) for their services! The Society was a forerunner of the many benefit societies of the 19th century, and in a way of the NHS, for members were insured if they fell ill, and could be paid up to seven shillings a week (35p) for a year. However the member would get nothing if he was hurt through gaming or any other unlawful activity, and he could not go to any public house while receiving benefit. The S.A.S continued to 1912 when it became a Lodge of the Independent Order of Oddfellows, and ran until 1972 when it became part of the Hook Norton Lodge. The annual service with a silver band took place up to 1987 when members plus visiting Oddfellows marched around the green behind the banner.

Sir John Betjeman, the famous Poet Laureate, who was familiar with all the churches of North Oxfordshire spoke in church at the annual service in 1971.

Staying in the south aisle there is a charming stained glass panel in a mullioned window which commemorates the 50th anniversary of the end of the 1939-45 war, with the doves of peace, an aeroplane and a cross.

Note the blocked up stairs by the chancel, and do not miss the partially obscured memorials in the floor by the altar to the Rev Edward Hughes and his wife Rebecca. Incidentally the Hughes family featured strongly as Rectors, from 1721 to 1846.

If ever the parable of the Good Samaritan bore fruit it did at Shenington, for there is a memorial to Samuel Davenport who left at his death in 1734 the sum of £120 to be distributed to the poor of Shenington plus £100 for the repair of the church. What Mr Hannah reveals however, is the story behind the bequest, for Samuel Davenport as a young man was destitute, and begged unsuccessfully for bread in nearby villages. Only in Shenington however, was he given food and shelter, and when he became an Alderman of the City of London in later life he remembered the village which helped him. He also remembered Robert and Elizabeth Pettipher (could they have been the people who helped him?) who died in their 80s in 1699 and 1713 by placing a memorial to them in the church.

Because the local stone is so soft there are few gravestones which can be dated but there is a memorial to Mary Good inside the church dated 1666.

Look at the base of one pillar to see an interesting face, and look up to the clerestory roof for some more jolly faces on the supports.

The very old church chest has three locks each with two keyholes, but it seems a bit near the tower stonework which is growing moss inside from leaking rainwater.

The simple octagonal font has a fine brassbound wooden bucket, and there is a commemorative notice in the porch by the Incorporated Society for Buildings and Churches dated 1879 which granted £15 for reseating and restoring and guaranteeing all seats for the free use of parishioners.

There's more to see in Shenington, but spare time for a walk down to St Michael's at Alkerton, the smaller, but similar church, perched on the hillside and while one always wonders at the craftsmanship of the builders all those years ago, one simply has to admire the skill and confidence of those who chose this site.

You come upon it almost by accident as it is hidden by trees and only accessible by steep steps from the road, or by walking past the Old Rectory off a tiny lane.

However it is very well cared for and remarkable because it has a high altar, up steps which transform a relatively small building into something quite impressive. Once again in Hornton stone, it appears to have been built on to the tower, and is unusual in that its windows are square-headed rather than rounded as at Shenington, which was far more usual in a mansion of the times rather than a church.

There are some fine carvings outside but sadly again they are heavily weathered, but there are some excellent colour pictures of them inside the church. Note the 12th century font, and a 13th century stone effigy of an unknown knight in armour in the chancel.

Alkerton has had its share of characters. Thomas Lydiat was born in 1572, went to Winchester and New College and was Chaplain to James I and tutor to the Prince of Wales. After the Prince's untimely death as a young man, Thomas' fortunes waned, and he became Rector at his home village in 1612. However after standing security to a friend he was imprisoned for debt from 1629 to 1632, and was closely acquainted with both the gaols at Banbury and Warwick! He used the time however to increase his reputation as a great scholar, and was referred to by Dr Johnson in 'The Vanity of Human Wishes'.

More venal was John Capel Townshend (1775-1821) who used to play whist in the Alkerton church porch while waiting for funerals.

First and best of the Rectors was probably Master William (1233-43) who was surgeon to Henry III.

Both Shenington and Alkerton have a wealth of historic riches in impressively hilly surroundings but allow an afternoon to fully enjoy them.

An unusual custom in Shenington is the annual strewing of grass in the church (Below). This probably dates from the middle ages, when the earthen floor would have been covered with rushes. These would have been changed once during the year and certainly in the spring. The custom has continued to the present day, with grass taking the place of the rushes. The Churchwarden's accounts record the strewing each year (1770 is the first year from which accounts survive,

earlier records having been burned in a disastrous fire in 1721). In the first half of the 18th century the cost of fetching the grass was 1/- (5p), but by the 1770's the rate had risen to 2/- (10p). The entry for 1773 reads, 'Fetching the grass at Whitsuntide and the Wakes 3/-'.

Village Wakes, the local annual festivals of an English village were held on the feast days of the patronal saint of the church. This fits in with the 1773 entry as the church is dedicated to the Holy Trinity and Trinity follows immediately after Whitsun.

As late as 1948, there was an annual village celebration with roundabouts and side shows on the village green on Trinity Monday. For many years this day was the annual meeting of the Oddfellows Club, with brass band, parade to church and a church service which always included the singing

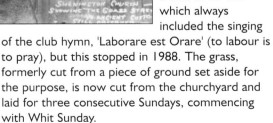

of the club hymn, 'Laborare est Orare' (to labour is to pray), but this stopped in 1988. The grass, formerly cut from a piece of ground set aside for the purpose, is now cut from the churchyard and laid for three consecutive Sundays, commencing with Whit Sunday.

Cropredy's concealed eagle & the shrine of St Fremund

In a recent episode of Cadfael on TV - that's the one where a monk is a Mediaeval detective - a Saint's bones were a highly valuable commodity which abbeys, cathedrals and parish churches prized highly, and whose clergy were prepared to lie and cheat to get them.

That is what might well have happened to poor old St Fremund, whose shrine was at St Mary the Blessed Virgin church at Cropredy. For St Fremund, who died in 866, was a martyr, and a relative of King Offa (he of the famous dyke) of Mercia, and of Edmund, King of East Anglia. Despite his royal connections he became a hermit, and because of his royal connections he was seen as a

possible claimant to the throne, and was killed by his kinsman, Oswy, with the help of the Danish army, who also slew King Edmund.

Supposedly originally buried at Offchurch, in Warwickshire, his relics were then transferred to Dunstable, where miracles attested to his sanctity. However, Cropredy claimed to have his body, and to this day there is a chapel to his memory; and in 1488, Richard Danvers of Prescote left 20 shillings in his will to the "repair of the chapel where his shrine is situated". St Fremund has his own Feast Day which is May 11th, although Cropredy's poor people would no doubt regard Christmas Eve as a better day because of 'Toms' Charity.'

'Tom' was not a man, but Mary Toms who died in 1896 and left £500 as 'Toms' Charity' with the income to be distributed to those who the Vicar and Churchwardens deemed worthy to have it, and who had lived in the village for at least ten years.

Just in case they might forget there is a tablet in the church which states: "This tablet should be affixed and maintained here: Not for the mere purpose of setting forth her charitable disposition and gift, but to the end that the persons for whose benefit the charity was constructed might be made aware of its existence and nature".

So if you are on your uppers in Cropredy it might be worth a call to the Vicar around

Christmas!

There was probably a church in Cropredy before the Norman Conquest, for the lower part of the south aisle dates from 1050, and there are two arched sepulchral recesses which are thought to be the

tombs of father and son, both Simon de Cropredy.

We know there were Roman vineyards at Horley, and it seems there may well have been vineyards around Cropredy as well, for vines appear on the wooden screens behind the choir, as well as the Tudor rose.

The sanctuary was often rebuilt, but the present one dates from the 14th century.

Most impressive however, are the wonderful perpendicular arches which dominate the church. The pillars rise with

their lines unbroken from the floor of the nave, and the arch to the tower has a bold and massive vaulted sweep to the roof.

Above the chancel arch are the remains of a doom wall painting, which was probably hidden in Puritan times.

Of course the history of Cropredy is inextricably tied up with the Civil War, and the battle of Cropredy Bridge in 1644. One can only imagine the fear and trepidation of the village when a Royalist vanguard took the bridge, only to be followed by the Cavalier army marching down one side of the River Cherwell, and Waller's Parliamentarians marching down the other to converge on Cropredy.

The church had, and luckily still has, a glorious pre-Reformation brass eagle lectern, but it was only due to the foresight of the congregation. Fearing a Puritan victory they hid it on the eve of the battle by plunging it into the Cherwell. It was unnecessary however, for the Royalists won the battle, but when it was retrieved from the river one of the three brass lions which formed the feet had disappeared. The poor old

• *The eagle lecturn which was recovered from the River Cherwell at Cropredy.*

eagle was so discoloured by the water that the replacement foot was made in bronze, and that can be seen today.

The twisted beak which gives the eagle a wry smile may have been used to collect Peter's Pence which was a tax paid to Rome. Coins were removed from a slot in the tail, but that has now wisely been soldered up!

A problem with all churches sadly is theft, and Cropredy's collection of Civil War armour was stolen from the church, but there is still a display case with armour in it. However the armour is only a replica given to commemorate the 350th anniversary of the battle, and is only of intrinsic value, but it shows what a soldier would have worn.

Nearby is a superb 13th century parish chest with three locks, one for the Vicar and one each for the two churchwardens and they could only be opened when all three were together. There is a tiny window above the vestry where the priest could look down on the congregations,

• *The pulpit which was roughly carved from the trunk of a Cropredy oak.*

and the remains of a door above the pulpit which led to the rood screen which disappeared years ago.

Not many monuments, but an interesting coat of arms in the chapel, a decorated plaque dated 1703, and two interesting modern memorials. They are to Richard Crossman, MP, teacher, writer and politician, a Minister in the Wilson government who died in 1975, and to a lovely gentleman who I always knew as 'the bee man". He was Maj Edward Donner, of Bourton House, who as well as being a churchwarden for a quarter of a century, kept bees and produced a particularly toothsome honey, and for that alone he deserved to be remembered.

• *The body armour is a replica of that worn at the time of the battle of Cropredy Bridge. It replaces the real armour which was stolen from the church. The original Norman font (left) which was returned to the church in 1914. There is another far more ornate decorated Victorian font which was acquired in 1853.*

South Newington's chamber of horrors

Depictions are lauded by many but prove too gruesome for some.

Where is Newton Jewel near Banbury? Don't know? Well try Newton Cranford. Still lost? Well, I have to admit that until I went to St Peter ad Vincula church I had no idea where they were either.

Now, however, I know that they were both 13th century names for South Newington, and the clues come from a bird in one of the windows in the church, a crane, which represented the Cranford family at that time.

All stained glass windows tell a story, and there's a lion in the east window in the south aisle which was on the shield of the aptly named William le Scissor, who was Henry III's tailor and who held land in the village. In the same window there is an eagle of the Buckland Shield, and in the south window there is a superb crimson heraldic shield.

But interesting as they are, they are nothing to the half severed head of Thomas of Lancaster, and the execution of Thomas a Becket, which are both part of some of the finest wall paintings of any church in Britain, and for which St Peter's is justly world renowned.

The church kindly invites the visitor to switch on the lights to see the glorious paintings in full colour at their best and if you do you will see them revealed in all their glory.

The current BBC Radio 4 series, The History of England recently told the story of the murder of Thomas in 1175 in gory detail, with one of the three knights sent by King Henry slicing off the crown of his head and revealing his brains. That moment, complete with blood spraying everywhere, is shown in this horror comic strip on the church wall.

What is particularly remarkable is that St Thomas' head has not been defaced - for King Henry VIII, in his battle with the church, ordered that all pictures of the Saint's head should be disfigured. This particular one escaped that fate as it had already been covered over with paint in the Middle Ages, and it is in fact one of only two in existence.

Next to the picture of the martyrdom however, is one which is unique, and equally as gory. And it involves our old acquaintance, Piers Gaveston, who was King Edward II's favourite and who was imprisoned at Deddington before being taken to Warwick and killed. For the man who killed him, and who led a rebellion against the King was Thomas of Lancaster, and it is his execution which is pictured here.

This painting is even more graphic than the Becket one, for poor old Lancaster had the bad luck to have an inexperienced axeman and it took several attempts to decapitate him. The hangman's frenzied efforts are captured in the frenzied sweep of the drawing and the upraised axe, and is totally blood chilling in this 'Goyaesque' painting.

However these remarkable pictures are not all blood and drama because there is one which many consider the finest.

Excellently preserved, it is the Virgin and Child framed in a gothic arch on a pedestal which has the three leopards of the Gifford family - the family which employed the anonymous talented artist who painted the

ET. VOCABITVR. AVLA. DEI.

19

• *Making a change from the gory events pictured elsewhere, The Virgin and Child.*

• *Thomas a Beckett has the top of his head sliced off 'exposing his brains'.*

pictures in the north aisle.

If you study nothing else, you cannot fail to be impressed by this example of the art of the time. Fascinatingly, the features of both Thomas Gifford and his wife Margaret Mortayne are featured in the depiction of the saints in the paintings - so they achieved immortality!

My favourite, however, is the picture of St Margaret, (not St George!) in the splay of a window slaying the dragon, for she is both beautiful and refined as she wields her lance.

These are the famous pictures, but in the nave, above two glorious sweeping Norman arches on massive carved pillars, are others, completed over a century later in a quite different, rustic style.

They show the Passion, and are once again in a strip along the wall, and equally absorbing. In fact there remain many paintings, especially a giant mural of the Last Judgement, painted

in the 14th century, like the executions, on the wall leading to the Chancel which remain to be restored. It is believed three quarters of this picture can be revealed again, and the church is currently working to raise money for this venture.

A hint of what it may be like can be seen next to the roof in the nave where there is a picture of the Virgin and St Michael weighing souls!

Artists will be intrigued to see that the - mid-14th century paintings, revealed in 1897, after being covered in lime and whitewash for centuries, are not frescoes but were executed in oil on plaster. Prof E.W.Tristram, who did an in-depth study of the murals in the 1930's, not only speaks of their religious importance, but emphasises their place in the history of art.

Apart from the murals and the miniature stained glass, St Peter's has a comparatively simple interior with no ornate memorials. But that is not to say it is uninteresting. For instance, someone over the years has collected the Royal Proclamations dating from the Charles II instruction in 1661 to mark the day of his father's execution (he calls it murder), with three from the reign of William and Mary demanding fast days - one to prevent and punish immorality and profaneness, and another from Queen Anne in 1706 marking a thanksgiving day. This was to celebrate Marlborough's victory over the 'boundless ambition of the French' at Brabant. The most recent is the Victory Proclamation by King George V, published in 1919.

The importance of the wool trade to the *Four Shires* area over the centuries is also recalled by proclamations and certificates for burying people in wool which was obligatory for a very long time.

Wool would also have been a reason for a Saxon

• *Lancaster is beheaded at the third try!*

settlement at South Newington, for shepherds from the West Country and the Cotswolds would have preferred to cross the River Swere to the south of the village on their way to Banbury.

The church was referred to in 1150, and has a fine simple Norman font, but it is an intriguing mixture of early decorated and perpendicular. The porch, with its six mini spires and amazing gargoyles is 14th century, and it has both a sundial and a niche which presumably had a statue of St Peter in chains, before the depredations of the Puritans, who probably also removed the statues from inside the church as well.

There are the remains of an early English cross leading to the porch, and the church tower with its arrow slit windows and battlements would have provided a fine defensive position to overlook the river crossing.

Famous families connected (however tenuously) with the church are of course, the Giffords, the Cranfords, the Ivals, the Mohuns and Claverings, and, much more recently, the Haringtons.

South Newington was referred to in a pre-Conquest document as Nivantun-meaning 'at the new settlement', but whether it was Nivantun, Newton Cranford, or Newton Jewel, its church has survived for nearly 1,000 years, and its paintings still show us living history in full Technicolor - and you can't get newer than that!

• *This ornate alabaster tomb houses the statues of Sir William Pope and his family including his faithful hounds!*

Wroxton Church, bassett hounds & St Judas

THE three wives of Wroxton must have been paragons of virtue if we are to believe the author of the monument in the village church of All Saints to the memories of Lucy, Elizabeth and Catherine, the spouses of Francis, 1st Earl of Guilford (1704-90).

The monument, one of many in this church of fine designs and carvings, is surmounted by three exquisitely simple white urns, but it pales in contrast to the magnificent tomb in the sanctuary to Sir William Pope, the builder of nearby Wroxton Abbey.

Carved in alabaster, he lies with his wife Anne, with their three children in a canopied bed surmounted by his coat of arms. He entertained King James I at the Abbey, and one wonders if that had anything to do with the fact that Charles I created him Earl of Downe.

Apparently the Pope family knew which side their bread was buttered for one of Sir William's immediate ancestors, Sir Thomas, was a friend of Henry VIII and was allowed to buy the monastery on the site of the present Abbey on the dissolution in 1536.

More famous by far than the Popes however were the Earls of Guilford linked to the Popes by marriage, and the most famous of these was Frederick, the second Earl, who is better known as Lord North, Prime Minister to George III during the American War of Independence which led to the loss of the British colonies in America, and later to the formation of the United States.

His tomb, which has the figure of Britannia plus a very friendly lion (his nose has been rubbed quite shiny by countless visitors) was carved by John Flaxman.

A sadder monument by far is that to another Pope - young Henry, who was just 19 years three months when he died of smallpox at Trinity College, Oxford. Trinity College of course was a great landowner in our area.

Most of the monuments in this church of monuments, are in the chancel, including a wall

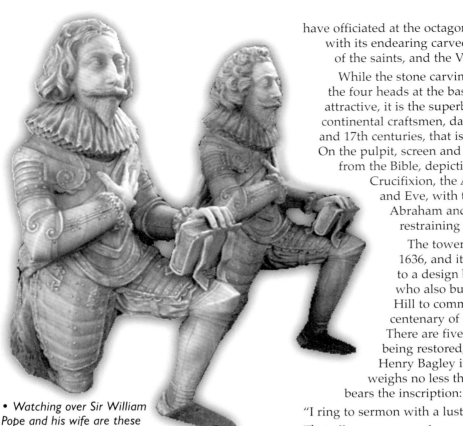

• *Watching over Sir William Pope and his wife are these two gentlemen.*

have officiated at the octagonal 14th century font with its endearing carved canopied figures of the saints, and the Virgin.

While the stone carving of the font and the four heads at the base of the arches are attractive, it is the superb wood carving, by continental craftsmen, dating from the 16th and 17th centuries, that is truly fascinating. On the pulpit, screen and chancel are scenes from the Bible, depicting the Nativity, the Crucifixion, the Ascension, Adam and Eve, with the tree and serpent, Abraham and Isaac and the restraining angel.

The tower was worked on in 1636, and it was rebuilt in 1748 to a design by Sanderson Miller who also built the tower at Edge Hill to commemorate the centenary of the Civil War battle. There are five bells, currently being restored, which were cast by Henry Bagley in 1676. The tenor weighs no less than 9 cwt, and No.5 bears the inscription:

"I ring to sermon with a lusty bome.

That all may come and none stay at home"

A massive organ loft dominates the west end of the church, and there is a piscina in the north aisle, but I particularly liked the little Victorian(?) stove under the base of the pulpit for which many a clergyman must have been grateful in winter.

I also found one part of the Victorian stained glass

tablet to Thomas Coutts, the London banker whose bank still bears his name and who had 'a life honourable to himself' and who was 'useful to all who engaged his friendship'.

One wall tablet on the north wall is touchingly different, for it is dedicated to commoner, Robert Innes, who died in 1857, and who was 'a faithful steward to Lt Col and Baroness North' who erected the memorial to him.

Just soaking up the history of England commemorated in the church can while away an hour or two, but so can the fabric of the present 14th century church. It was built on the site of a church that existed at least as early as 1217, with Michael Belet as Rector, who founded an Augustinian priory.

In 1226 John de Compton (a well known local name) was incumbent, while Johannes Banbury held the benefice in 1504, and must

• *Some of the beautiful carving on the pulpit for which the church is justly famed.*

windows intriguing for it is dedicated to St Judas, who, I, in my ignorance expected to be reviled rather than honoured.

I have always liked Wroxton, firstly because I took my very first photograph with a Box Brownie during the 1939-45 war on a visit to the abbey, and secondly because I have long kept basset hounds as pets, and that has endeared at least one member of the North family to me. For I was once told that one of the Norths kept a pack of bassets for hunting on foot, and in 22 years never caught anything, neither fox, hare or rabbit.

They were, I was reliably informed, kept - "to give his Lordship some regular exercise", and their performance in the field was immaterial.

I am not in the least surprised!

The Earl and his wives

Francis, 1st Earl of Guilford (1704-90) outlived three wives, and he must have been singularly lucky in his choice, for he loved all three equally well.

First was Lucy, who died in 1734 aged 25, second was Elizabeth who died in 1745 aged 38, and third was Katherine who died in 1766 aged 52.

Their combined epitaph reads thus:

"These excellent wives possessed every good quality which characterises a sincere Christian. Their providence and affability commanded universal esteem and respect. Their delight was in doing good. The distressed of every kind who desired their assistance had always reason to be satisfied. They raised their husband to a degree of happiness far beyond what man ought to expect in this mortal state and added proofs at their death of their sincere affection and esteem.

Nothing but the power of Divine Providence inspiring Christian resignation could have enabled him to support the excruciating grief on being deprived of them.

The world cannot sufficiently lament their loss. Their bright examples call aloud for imitation."

• *The carved effigies of Sir William Pope with his wife, Anne, lie in state.*

Betjeman's Church, Adderbury

• The wooden ceiling at St Mary's which rises high above the pews.

Who was W.F.Wilton? I ask because while visiting St Mary's Church at Adderbury I came across his name under the evocative St George and the dragon 1914-19 war memorial, and as I had always believed we were the only Wiltons around locally, I would dearly love to know who our namesake was. Perhaps someone knows and can tell me?

Enough of personal matters and on to this glorious church. If Middleton Cheney is the church of windows, then St Mary's is the church of statues, but much more than that it is as near a cathedral as one could hope to find in a village - even in a village whose former inhabitants included the Earl of Rochester, and Lord Charles Montague, who was William III's Chancellor of the Exchequer.

While the nave of the church dates back to 1250, this is a building that is clearly well cared for, with a sound system, glass doors for the tower, fresh sweet smelling flowers (clearly there is no silly superstition about having lilac indoors!), and a 1995

inset in the south aisle window commemorating a millennium.

Accustomed to seeing ancient memorials it was good to see the ornate plaque commemorating Col Henry Everard DuCane Norris, whose mastiff once placed his paws on my shoulders and gave me not only a massive fright but a good wash with his tongue, before the Colonel's death in 1960. Col Norris was High Sheriff, and Vice Lieutenant of Oxfordshire, and served with the Royal Warwicks in the South African war, and with the Royal Naval division in the 1914-18 war. He was also a Knight of the Order of St John, and had close connections with the local St John Ambulance Brigade.

Not quite as imposing is the memorial to Sir Edward Grasett who died in 1971. He was Lt Governor of Jersey and Colonel Commandant of the Royal Engineers.

Fiennes is of course the family name of the Saye and Sele family at Broughton Castle, but I had not seen it used as a Christian name until I saw the sad little memorial to Fiennes, 3rd son of Robert Eddowes and Susanna, who died in 1723, aged just six months.

I must say I was very taken by another memorial to John and Elizabeth, and Jane the wife of Antoni, who was John's son and heir, for Elizabeth had no fewer than 17 children,

and Jane bore 11 youngsters. John died in 1534 and Elizabeth and Jane in 1568. Whoever chose the text - "they do rest from theyr labours" must have had a sense of humour.

The chancel with its 14 statues behind the

altar, all around 18 inches tall, and its elegant traced hoods over the Virgin and the Angel Gabriel was built by Richard Winchcombe and not by William of Wykeham, Bishop of Winchester, whose bust is outside the east window, along with corbel stones of Edward III. Other window corbel stones show winged angels holding shields, a bearded man and an angel, an old woman blowing bellows on to a fire beneath a cauldron, a man with a sack, and a shepherd shearing sheep.

In his 'Story of Adderbury Church', the Rev J.P.Vyvan records that the exterior of the church is noted for its carvings of the Early English characters, with on the north and south sides friezes of grotesque figures, and a series representing musicians with old-time instruments such as a portable organ, a timbrel, the bagpipes, a hurdy gurdy, a psaltry, a harp, a violin, a trumpet, and kettle drums.

Obviously music was appreciated in Mediaeval times, and that tradition continues with the melodious tunes from the bells timed by the clock with quarter chimes to commemorate Queen Victoria's diamond jubilee in 1897. I was there on a Wednesday so I enjoyed the Bluebells of Scotland - but there are a further six different tunes for the other days of the week.

Watch out for the brasses of a knight and his wife in the south transept, the mixed 17th and 18th century tombstones in the floor, the 16th and 17th century stones lining the path by the church, the 13th century tiles discovered in 1936 in the south transept, the superb 14th century ironwork on the chest, and the two beautifully slender square fluted pillars in the north and south aisles which contrast with the later sturdier octagonal pillars of the nave.

There are more gargoyles, corbel faces, and animals than you can shake a stick at in this cruciform church; a particularly attractive

• *The St George war memorial.*

lych gate, a very large churchyard leading down to Sor Brook crammed full of gravestones marking four centuries, and some particularly fine, late, perpendicular windows.

I came away with the impression that I had only skimmed the surface of what can be enjoyed at this church and Poet Laureate, John Betjeman, wrote of St Mary's in 1958: "The tower and spire and the windows make its exterior about the finest in the country".

Few would quarrel with that.

The healthiest place in *The Four Shires?*

Newbottle must be the healthiest place in Banburyshire. Why? Because if we use the rule that lichens will only flourish where the air is pure then ironically the churchyard at Newbottle, which boasts no fewer than 91 different varieties, must top the clean air list.

We know that the lichens are there because of the work of Tom Chester in 1988 when he not only identified the vast number of lichens, but also one, bacidia fuscoviridis, which holds the record for being the first to appear in any British habitat,

with the only other of its kind occurring in Connemara West Ireland.

Tom was only able to carry out his survey because the churchyard of this, one of the smallest of Banburyshire's churches, has been a nature reserve for the past 18 years, and was commended by the Wildlife Trust of Northamptonshire in 1997.

And, as well as the lichens, it has such fascinating plants as birdsfoot trefoil, hairy buttercress, common mouse ear, hairy violet and bird's eye speedwell, while in the air above the re-built 14th century church fly three varieties of owl, four different finches, and three woodpecker varieties plus a kestrel and sparrowhawk.

A colony of bees has also lived in the tower.

When I visited Newbottle in January there were already masses of snowdrops among the old headstones - there have been no new burials there for nearly 80 years - and the church, in a tree lined cul de sac, was a haven of absolute peace. Genial Scotsman, Ian Luke, saw me looking at the church and very kindly produced the key to let me have a look round.

The hamlet contains the Manor House, and a couple of other dwellings, although once it was bigger than nearby Charlton. Now however St James is Charlton's church, and it

29

• *The original early English lancet windows with their infilled Victorian stained glass windows.*

has an interesting past. Canon Michael Hayter tells us both Charlton and Purston had chapels of ease in the past but both have disappeared without trace.

There was a church in Norman times, and the tower, and probably the barrel shaped font are all that remains of that building. Some time between 1147 and 1167 William de Pinu, Lord of Newbottle Manor assigned it to the Priory of Dunstable, which appointed vicars to serve it.

Within 100 years however all except the tower was demolished, and the present church was rebuilt in the 14th century.

The nave windows are all much later than the main structure, although the charming early English lancet windows remain in the chancel. There are few mediaeval materials or furnishings, but there is a good 16th century brass in the north wall of the sanctuary to Peter Dormer, successor to Sir Michael Dormer of Purston who bought the rectorial tithes when Dunstable Priory was dissolved by Henry VIII. He is pictured with his two wives and 19 children!

The Dormers were followed by the Creswells, and there is a large memorial dated 1655, to John Creswell and his wife, Elizabeth. John had a fiery temper, and when his wife produced yet another daughter after giving birth to several other girls, he threw the new baby down the stairs and killed her. There is a baby angel in his memorial and this may have been the reason.

He fought for the King in the Civil War, and eventually met his just reward when he was killed in a duel.

The church was extensively restored in 1856 when the present choir stalls and pews were installed. Previously, big box pews were reserved for Newbottle Manor, Purston, Charlton Lodge, Astrop, the Vicarage and Charlton farmers, and there were open benches for servants of the big houses, and the rest were free.

Final re-roofing of the church took place as recently as 1984.

Inside the church the stairway leading to the top of the rood screen is still complete, and the 1584 pulpit has the initials FBV inlaid.

In the north aisle is a mediaeval Spanish chest which has a double lid and Canon Hayter records: "It was brought from

Spain with the more elaborate of the sanctuary chairs, by the Earl of Birkenhead. The chest has a double lid, and the outer lid, when raised, shows a painted head of Christ, which may mean that it was designed to be a portable altar."

The great law lord, F.E.Smith, Earl of Birkenhead, lived in the parish but is buried in Charlton graveyard, where his elder daughter, the novelist, Lady Eleanor Smith who wrote some absorbing and exciting novels of gypsy life, is also buried.

For those, like me, who find war memorials compulsive, the simple memorial includes the names of 18 parishioners who died in the 1914-18 war - four from the Oxfordshire and Buckinghamshire LI, one from the Queen's Own Oxfordshire Hussars, and one who served with the Canadian Force. Four parishioners died in the 1939-45 war.

On the exterior of the church are carved heads above a stained glass window, and a sundial dated 1764 which was restored in 1975 as a memorial to Mary Harper of Charlton.

David Morgan who is a lay reader at the church, which has been united with King's Sutton since 1988, tells me a new incumbent has been appointed but is not likely to be inducted for another three months. In the meantime, regular Sunday services are taken by visiting clergymen.

Perhaps one will go on to repeat the success of one mid-18th century curate, the Rev John Moore, who went on in 1783 to become Archbishop of Canterbury!

Middleton Cheney's world famous glass

I am ashamed to say that having lived in Middleton Cheney for the past 13 years I have seldom visited the beautiful All Saints Church, which attracts people from all over the world for its glorious windows.

The work of Edward Burne-Jones, Ford Madox Browne, William Morris, and Philip Webb are all represented in the stained glass masterpieces.

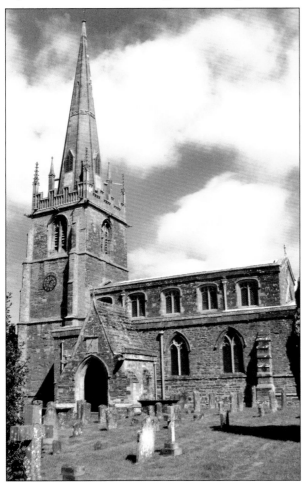

'The Tribes of Israel' and 'Abraham and Moses' were designed by orthodox Jew, Simeon Solomon, who was working in stained glass for William Morris and Co for the one and only time.

While the superb windows with their hints of the Pre-Raphaelite movement, are the jewel in the crown, the church and indeed its graveyard would be well worth a visit even if (Heaven forbid) they were not there.

The Perpendicular spire soars over the old part of the village and at around 150 feet dominates the skyline on the the northern slopes of the Cherwell Valley rivalling King's Sutton and Bloxham.

Like King's Sutton, the church has suffered from the fall of two of the eight pinnacles which came through the roof in 1990, causing damage and replacement costs which amounted to over £40,000!

Only a year away from being a 13th century church, the main structure of the church was built by William de Edyngton (later Bishop of Winchester), in 1301 to replace a 12th century edifice.

Before entering the church through the 696 year old door, it's worth looking at the impressive recently-restored Horton tomb, which commemorates, both Mary Ann Horton who died in 1969, and her father and mother, William and Elizabeth Horton of Highbury Grove in Middlesex, who both died in September 1833.

William, who was Lord of the Manor, died on the 23rd aged 80, and his wife just two days after - from a broken heart? And if the name Horton sounds familiar, it should, for as well as financing almshouses in the

village, the family gave its name to the Horton Hospital in Banbury.

Look round a little further and on the north side of the graveyard is a headstone to Arthur Webb Mold, who played cricket for Lancashire and England. He died in 1921 aged 55, and the stone was erected 'by old cricketing friends as a token of their affection, admiration and respect'.

If you are there late at night you might well hear the clash of swords, pikes and muskets, for several of Oliver

Cromwell's civil war Parliamentarian soldiers who died in a skirmish in 1643 near the new by-pass, are buried in the churchyard.

Once inside the church, feast your eyes on the windows, and pick up for a few pence the excellent comprehensive description of the stained glass by 1994 Churchwarden, Mrs Irene Forrest.

But spare time too for the fine painted 15th century clerestory ceiling last painted in 1865 by Mr Cottam, of

Banbury, working under the direction of Sir Gilbert Scott. Note too the masks at the foot of the arches which are clever cartoons in sculpture and probably based on members of the congregation in 1460.

Above all a church of visual delights, there are two interesting mosaics which would benefit from spotlighting to bring out the many facets of the glass in them.

It's a wonder how the delicate woodwork in the choir stalls has survived over the years, but survive it has, to charm the choristers and visitors alike.

Not a church with many memorials, there is one recent one which like most for those who fell in the 1914-18 war is particularly poignant.

It is to Ernest George de Lathom Hopcraft, only son of Ernest Hopcraft, who was a Northants JP. Aged 32 he 'answered duty's call, volunteered and was commissioned in the 13th Middlesex Regt. He gave his life, his all for King and Country. After having fought in Palestine he fell in action at the assault on the German Hindenburg Line at Marcuoy, near Cambrai, after gallantly attacking a German machine gun post single-handedly, just five weeks and four days before the Armistice'.

Middleton Cheney also had its share of generous people in the past for Richard Garnett

• The Horton Memorial.

who originally came from Lancashire left £1,000 in 1764 to ornament the chancel, and either £50 or £150 for the poor of the Parish - it's a little difficult to sort out the last piece of his memorial.

John Barkesdale, who died in 1701, was 'of ancient extraction' but had no heirs, and left his estate to a lucky namesake, John Barkesdale of Cirencester. He too left £20 to the poor of the Parish forever, and £20 then was a great deal of money.

So how did a village church like Middleton Cheney get such superb windows?

Well, since 1658 the living has been held by Brasenose College, Oxford, and in the 1860's the incumbent was William Buckley, Fellow of the College, and he was a friend of both Sir Edward Burne Jones, and Sir Gilbert Scott. They were part of a group of artists and must have enjoyed vying with each other to design the many separate scenes in the windows.

Leave the church by the 'semi-detached' porch with its unequal sides, and wonder at its tall pointed roof which is made of stone supported by three interlocking beams.

George Walker in his finely illustrated book 'Churches of the Banbury Area' said the then Rector told him it was a type of construction using no timber which was only found at the sister church of Chacombe, and at Corby.

Wild Bill and the King of Norway!

DID 'Wild' Bill come from Fritwell? Or rather did his family originate from the village and move to the USA? One wonders because on the chancel wall in St Olave's church at Fritwell there is a brass plate marking the remains of William Hickock which reads: "Here lyeth buried the body of William Hickock who departed this life the 8th of September, Anno Domini 1638, who after the decease of Philip (sic) his wife hath given 40 shillings by the year for ever unto the poore of Fruitwell to be paid by those that possess the land".

Of course it's only a coincidence that our Oxfordshire Bill had the same name, but the brass plaque is interesting on its own account, not only for the presumed misspelling of his wife's name (Phillippa surely), but because the engraver managed to turn Fritwell into Fruitwell, and had to split words, and use tiny end letters to make the lines fit. It's a bit of fun to count all the oddities, so give it a try.

In any case it's a bit rich of a 21st century writer to make a joke of strange spellings for it's only in recent years that spelling has become in any way standardised.

For instance Fritwell was traditionally 'Fyrht-welle' in Saxon times, and was two settlements built around two manor estates dedicated to St Frideswide, the patron saint of Oxford City and the University.

Then after the Norman Conquest the name changed to Fertewell and the village lands were given by William the Conqueror to his half brother Odo. In turn he gave them to Wadard his steward and chief huntsman. Most people know that the Normans took their name from Norsemen (the Vikings) so it was no surprise that the Fritwell Normans dedicated their new

• The massive organ, pictured here, dominates the church interior and is a remarkable memorial to Hannah Mary Hopcraft.

church to St Olaf (or Olave) the patron saint of Norway, who was both the Christian King of Norway, and a Viking warrior.

The church itself, despite massive re-building in the late 19th century retains some superb Norman work – the original chancel arch with its zig zag carving was moved to form an alcove, and the carved stone south doorway is especially interesting.

The north door is the one in normal use, but you can get into the south porch from inside the church by lifting the latch and turning the rimlock. Then you will see the remarkable carving on the Norman arch with ball and zig zag chevron moulding, plus a relief of two beasts feeding on each side of a tree. The tree symbolises the tree of life or knowledge and is said to be 'an exhortation to all who enter the church to follow the beasts' example and devour the Christian precepts that the church teaches'.

• *A quiet corner in the south aisle of the church bathed in late September sunlight.*

Proof that the porch itself is much later than the doorway comes from two scratch dials, one on each side of the doorway carved to show villagers the four main times for prayers during the day. They were later obscured from the sunlight by the porch and became useless.

The north door is also Norman with cable moulding, but the grotesque animal heads are now almost eroded away.

Pictures inside the present church show that it was once a fine 12th century building with 15th century additions, but by the mid 19th century it had deteriorated so much that it was declared unfit and unsafe for public use and looked for a while as if it would be abandoned.

However, the Rev Samuel Yorke bought the Manor and the living of St Olave's and became the Vicar. Obviously not wanting to be a Vicar with a tumbledown church he generously personally commissioned major restoration at a cost of £2,000 – a very sizable sum in those days.

The architect was G.E.Street, who studied with Gilbert Scott and worked with William Morris and the pre-Raphaelite group of artists and craftsmen, and whose work included the impressive London Law Courts. Morris, of course, greatly influenced the stained glass installed in Middleton Cheney church.

Street ensured that the original faulty castellated mediaeval tower was rebuilt with a pyramid roof, and the low nave roof which had clerestory windows was replaced with a steeper pitched roof. A coke fired boiler provided under floor heating and there's a smart chimney near the north door to take the smoke away.

He also designed the stunning round stone pulpit, the cross and reredos behind the high altar. The fine black wrought iron chancel screen was probably made by a local craftsman however, who one suspects made the elegant lectern as well.

What makes the church interior so unusual however is the immense organ loft, organ and vestry screen in the west end which looms some 20 feet high above the pews. It was built following a kind bequest from Hannah Mary Hopcroft, and houses a two-manual organ built by H.S.Vincent and Co of Sunderland.

The organ loft is so dominant that it tends to overshadow the fine four Norman arcades on either side of the nave, the south side pillars with round capitals and the north with octagonal ones.

There are four bells in the key of B flat and a Sanctus bell in the restored tower – a 1949 treble by Mears and Stainbank, the second bell (1612) and the tenor (1618) by Robert Atton and the third (1865) by George Mears. Repairs to the bells were carried out by the ubiquitous Whites of Appleton in 1991.

• *Pictured above is the 13th century octagonal font with its ogee decoration.*

Two years later the entire nave roof was renewed using new Cotswold slates, and the chancel roof was restored in 1994, using re-cycled stone slates.

Don't miss the unusual Norman pillar piscina with a crocket capital in the chancel and the 13th century octagonal font decorated with ogee headed panels.

There's no doubt that Fritwell (like all our *Four Shires* villages) was deeply affected by the deaths of their men in two World Wars, and they made certain that the six Great War soldiers, two from the Oxf and Bucks LI, two from Royal Warwicks, from the Machine Gun Corps and the Royal Field Artillery would not be forgotten. There's a fine wooden memorial in the church with carved crossed rifles and bayonets, but the really spectacular memorial is the impressive lych gate which was given by Sir John Allsebrook, afterwards the 1st Viscount Simon, Lord High Chancellor who lived at the Manor House (Fritwell) from 1911 to 1932, and his wife Kathleen. It's a lovely structure and a fine memorial too to the generosity of Lord Simon.

Ralph was the first incumbent in 1160 when the living was in the gift of St Frideswide's Priory, and it remained in the Priory's gift until 1347 until King Edward III became the patron to Nigel Broun. The final royal connection was in 1532 when Henry VIII gave the living to Nicholas Tarleton.

But of course the main royal connection is with St Olaf (or Olave) for he was quite a man.

JVM who has written the invaluable and very informative church notes tells us that Olaf Haroldsson was just 12 when he was first sent on a raiding trip to the Baltic. He proved so proficient that by 1012 he was a mercenary helping Ethelred the Unready who was in danger of losing London to a large force of Danes attacking across London Bridge from their base in Southwark.

Olaf and his men erected protective plank shields over their ships, lashed ropes round the wooden bridge piles and rowed their hardest downstream – pulling down the bridge structure and drowning many Danes in the process. This audacious exploit inspired the song 'London Bridge is Falling Down' – which was news to me.

After this, he came to power as King Olaf of Norway when he was 21, converted the Norwegians to Christianity, and was eventually killed in battle against a combined Danish and Norwegian force four times the size of his own army.

He was buried in a sandbank at Nidaros near Trondheim but soon miraculous healing powers from the site were soon reported, and a Bishop Grimkell had his body dug up where it was found to be perfectly preserved. Olaf was proclaimed a Saint and Martyr in 1031, and his cult spread throughout Europe.

He was credited with numerous miracles – but perhaps the biggest one is how a fine church in a pretty Oxfordshire village still bears the name of a great Norwegian king.

• *Pictured above is how the church looked before its restoration when it lost its castellated tower and its clerestory windows.*

Hook Norton's Star Signs
Mysterious symbols can be seen at St Peter's, Hook Norton

If you are an Aquarian you should stay away from St Peter's Church, Hook Norton, unless you have a thick skin, and do not mind being considered the evil one!

For almost as soon as you get inside you will see the carved Norman font which has your birth sign, the water carrier, being driven away by Sagittarius, the archer. The symbolism apparently is that the archer is driving away evil, since Aquarius was deemed to be responsible for the flood.

The font dates from 1100 AD, and also has the pictures of Adam and Eve, Aries the ram and supposedly a two headed serpent, which the expert who writes about the font believes has one head biting the other, which depicts the self destructive power of evil. The only problem with this explanation however is that one of the serpent's heads has ears, and the legs of a horse!

Everyone will no doubt have their own opinion, but apart from the unusual aspect of having signs of the zodiac on the font in the first place, the actual carving of Adam alongside a strange design strongly resembles the drawings of the Incas in Peru, which gives us another mystery.

And just who was the lady whose bust is hidden away at the back of the church on the floor behind a pew - and what had she done to be exiled there?

Apart from these mysteries however, the church is very open and spacious and it took me some time to realise just why. There is no rood - screen that disappeared in the 1850's, so there is no obstruction to hide one of the only two stained glass windows, and the plastered chancel is painted sparkling white.

Then I realised - there are no wooden choir stalls, they have been replaced by light individual oak choir seats with prayer rests which can be easily placed anywhere in the church.

With the comparatively newly installed light wood parquet flooring reaching out into the nave, the church is now a skilful mixture of the ancient and the new.

Ancient because there is evidence that the chancel was originally part of a Saxon Minster. Later, in 1129, the church came into the possession of the Augustinian abbey at Osney.

• *Just what is this? It's described as a two headed serpent, but the one on the left clearly has ears, and the forelegs of a horse.*

The first incumbent in 1224 was simply known as Hugh, and between 1300 and 1349 the Rector was William of Bannebury, and up to the Reformation there were ten knights who held the benefice. Another special link with Banbury is the chancel window dedicated to the Rev John Rushton who was 11 years Curate of Banbury and then 40 years incumbent at St Peter's. The only other stained glass window commemorates those who died from the village in the 1914-18 war.

The ring of eight bells was recast in 1949, and they commemorate the dead of the 1939-45 war, with the treble dedicated to Margaret Dickens, the author of 'A History of Hook Norton'. Until recent times the bells were rung every Guy Fawkes day as they had been since 1606. They were also rung in 1733 for the wedding of the Prince of Orange, and Anne, daughter of George II.

There are eight magnificent pinnacles on the tower suitably topped with pennant weather vanes, renewed by members of the crew of HMS Sultan in the Royal Navy.

While the interior of the church lacks the fine monuments of many other churches around Banbury, it does have the remains of some remarkable murals which covered the walls until the Reformation, when many of the statues, both inside and outside the church were probably destroyed as well.

There is one interesting

Elizabethan monument to John Croker of 'Hoke' Norton, and a grave slab with an inscription to Isabel de Plesset, widow of a 13th century Lord of the Manor, who was a successor to Robert D'Oily, who was a great builder and who probably built the Norman part of the church.

If you visit St Peter's, first of all buy the excellent guide to the churches of Hook Norton, Swerford and Great Rollright, and then look out for the illuminated cross behind the altar, a blocked-in sedilia, believed to be one of the oldest in the country, the Royal Arms, the corbels in the roof with their intriguing faces, the 1727 oak chest, and of course, that mysterious font.

Poor old Hooky has been getting a bit of stick from the CPRE recently, but the church with its energetic and popular Rector, and its modernisation (there is even a system for the hard of hearing) seems to be a nucleus for growing activity.

• *The Royal Arms over the church door.*

• WW 1777 and TH 1787 - did the scratcher return after ten years away or were they different people? We'll never know for sure. (Pictured right - the church key)

Chacombe's 18th Century graffiti at SS Peter and Paul

IF you thought that graffiti was a comparatively modern phenomenon, then think again. For while today's paint sprayers have undoubtedly used aerosol technology for their pastime, graffito, as it is properly termed, was regularly seen in medieval churches, and there are two fine examples of the 'scratcher's' art in the church of SS Peter and Paul at Chacombe. Both in two pillars of the 14th century church, one shows a bishop wearing a mitre, and the other is a head. While these are

mediaeval, there are initials in the porch 'WW 1777', and 'TH 1787' which must have passed away an hour or so for the perpetrators.

They are not easy to find however, and that is typical of the mysteries in this spacious, light and unadorned building with its white walls, and arcades.

Indeed one of the most exciting for me was only re-discovered in 1989 when stones from a previously blocked up window were removed to reveal a wall painting in great detail of St

40

Peter being crucified upside down.

The massive rectangular stone that was above the wall is now back in use as a medieval altar identified by the consecration crosses on the surface and the hole in which a relic would have been hidden.

One of the great revelations in visiting local churches has been the wealth of material that dedicated church members have amassed over the years, and then distilled into guides for visitors. To date the best of these is the one on sale at Chacombe for just £1, written by Betty D. Cameron which is perfect for casual visitor and serious student alike.

For as well as detailing the charms of the church, the guide tells of Chacombe in the Domesday Book, with the Bishop of Lincoln having land for ten ploughs, four slaves (!), 20 villagers and nine smallholders, plus three mills.

A century later, Hugh de Chaucombe founded nearby Chacombe Priory for Augustinian canons, dedicated to St Peter and St Paul, and as early as the 12th century there was a Vicar of Chacombe, and his church was probably Anglo Saxon.

Chacombe was also famous for its bell foundry from 1600 to 1785 and one of the interesting gravestones is one to Henery (sic) Bagley 'who departed this life on the first day on January 1683/4. To perpetuate the memory of an ingenious bell founder this stone was repaired 1796'. In 1732 Henry Bagley Junior published a catalogue of 441 bells already cast by the family, including ten for Lichfield Cathedral'. One wonders if they could have obtained local ironstone for their bells, for plenty of opencast ore was mined at Wroxton as recently as the 1960's.

With its white lime washed walls reflecting the light from the clerestory windows, the only splash of colour comes from the east window given in 1930 by the Cornwallis family who lived at the Priory.

• *Revealed in 1989 when stones were removed, this picture of St Peter being crucified upside down.*

At the other end of the church are the remains of some much older glass. Remains, because the window was damaged on the night of the massive bombing raid on Coventry in winter 1940, when it was believed that a lone German plane jettisoned two bombs over the village. On that night Banbury people standing at the top of the Oxford Road hill could see the blaze from the city in the sky.

It's worth taking a walk around the church to

see how the building changed over the years. There are clear signs (to me at any rate) of straight pitched arches which seem much older than the 13th century. There's a fine restored church clock dated 1739, and a stone sundial.

Another hint of an earlier church is the fine circular early Norman font, and the ubiquitous carved heads which abound in Banburyshire churches. Chacombe has a fine collection.

The way the walls in the chancel lean outwards is no optical illusion, but the result is attractive to the eye.

Staying in the chancel there are memorials to the Fox family with the arms of the City of London, and of the Grocers' company, and to William Armistead, the 18th century vicar, who was 'loving to his family, liberal to the needy, kind to the fatherless, and widows, and thus with his accounts ready left this world in love and peace with all mankind'.

Betty Cameron invites visitors to stand on the seat to the east of the organ in the chancel, to see an old tombstone which has been used to make a window ledge, and which has this inscription: "From thy quick death Conclude we must ....But as she says, the rest is tantalisingly missing.

Fascinating to see among the Vicars, the name Loggin (well known in Charlton), Robert de Wardington, Richard Ricote of Somerton, Francis Wykeham Martin, and on a tomb in the churchyard, Fiennes (some Broughton connection surely) Cornwallis, a survivor of the Charge of the Light Brigade in the Crimea in 1854.

The famous Pevsner writes about the church, but pride of place must go to Betty Cameron who writes: "As you have explored the church in its beautiful, peaceful, rural setting, I hope that you have felt the tranquillity and spirituality of centuries of worship in a building treasured and preserved throughout its long history".

Sentiments with which I wholeheartedly concur, along with many others who have written similar comments in the church Visitors' Book.

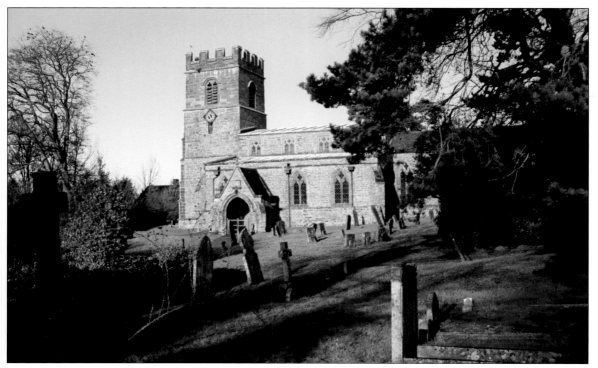

Aynho Church - the casualty of many wars

Rosemary is for remembrance and every year someone unknown goes into St Michael's church at Aynho and puts a spray of fresh rosemary on a plaque in memory of two brothers who were killed in the 1914-18 war.

The brothers were both 20, both served as 2nd Lieutenants in the Durham Light Infantry, and both were killed at Ypres. They were the sons of the Rev William Digby Cartwright who was Rector from 1906 to 1926, and the eldest died in 1915, only to be followed by his younger brother who was killed in battle in 1917.

The inscription reads: "Lovely and pleasant in their lives in their death they were not divided".

They followed in a great family military tradition as the splendid memorial plaques on the church walls record.

It is a roll call of British history in the past century for General William Cartwright fought with the 61st Foot, the Third Dragoons, and the 10th Hussars in the Peninsular Wars and at Waterloo.

His second son, Aubrey Agar was a Captain in the Rifle Brigade (the regiment that is now linked with the old Oxford and Bucks Light Infantry and the Royal Greenjackets) and he fought at Alma and Balaclava in the Crimea, only to fall at Inkerman. He 'fell pierced with balls in the act of bravely encouraging the young riflemen to stand firm', aged 29.

His elder brother Fairfax, born in 1823, had a longer and more exotic military career, joining Archduke Charles' Regiment of Lancers in the Austrian Army in 1848. He was then commissioned in the British Army and served as a Major with the German Legion in the Crimea. He later became MP for the Southern Division of Northants.

Visitors to this remarkable hybrid church have to get the massive main door key from the genial Geoff Stevens, who has been churchwarden for 36 years, or from his charming wife. The other long serving churchwarden is William Usher.

The church is hybrid, for all that remains of the original early 14th century building is the tower, which like so many churches in the Banbury area has niches which once held statues of saints before the depredations of the Puritans in the Civil War. A dragon's tail is all that is left above the west door.

The Royalists were equally destructive for they burned down the fine mansion adjoining the church during their retreat from Naseby in 1645. The war caused immense damage to the church and the main building apart from the tower was demolished and rebuilt in 1723 in the present imposing Grecian style, designed by Edward Wing. Wing came from Aynho and designed many similar London churches.

I found the church a revelation on two counts. First, it was amazingly warm, on one of the coldest days of the year, and secondly it was so spacious, and so unlike most village churches.

Like St Mary's at Banbury it has a gallery (which can hold 50 people) reached by two curved staircases, but it has no chancel, but box pews. It is also light and airy, mainly due to the light ceiling which replaced a dark wooden ceiling, which itself had replaced a white plaster interior.

As well as the plaques, there are some fine monuments by the altar, but the most interesting has to be the wooden one on the wall, underneath the gallery which was 'a carving of Christ, given by King Louis XIII to the Sisters of the Hospital of St Louis' to put in their chapel. It was given by the Cartwrights in memory of Richard Cartwright and his son, Edward, who were tragically killed in a car accident in 1954. Their death ended the Cartwright connection with Aynho Park, which is now split into apartments.

The carving shows in the background the Hospital begun in Henry IV's reign and finished in King Louis' in 1619.

Although the tower, with its large off centred clocks and fine decorated window, dates from Edward III, there was clearly a Norman church pre-dating it, for the first incumbent was Ralf de Didacto who died in 1210. There was probably a Saxon church as well, for the village was held in Edward the Confessor's name by Asgar, his standard bearer, who was a Saxon Thane in 1043. All the incumbents' names are recorded forever carved into the stone floor of the main aisle.

Items to look out for are the Georgian pulpit, the superb carving of a pelican which is the lectern, the organ with its decorated pipes, the fine hassocks, and, of course, the unusual stained glass windows with 19th century artistic designs.

Pick up the excellent illustrated booklet (just 50p) by children from the Aynho C of E school which is a first class guide, and if you are lucky enough to be at the church at either 9am, 12 noon, 3pm or 6pm you will hear the tunes from the carillon, which include the Bluebells of Scotland (Thursday) and Home Sweet Home (Saturday), as well as famous hymns.

Wander round the large churchyard and you will see the stepped stone cross which probably stood elsewhere in the village, and which was a meeting point for villagers when wandering preachers and pilgrims visited the area.

St Michael's is a strange church architecturally, but do not be put off by its grandly ornate classical exterior. Inside it is exceptionally clean, welcoming and obviously a working church, with the strangely touching tiny chairs under the gallery for the children who are so clearly loved and nurtured.

The first time I fell in love was on VE Day, 1945. The girl's name was Joyce, and she was the daughter of the cook at Broughton Castle, and her mother was steaming asparagus at the time.

Ever since, asparagus has been my favourite vegetable either with plain butter or sauce Hollandaise and Broughton has been my favourite local village!

While I was waiting for Joyce, having cycled from Banbury, I used to pop into the church to see the painted tomb of the builder, Sir John de Broughton who died in 1315.

In his multi coloured tunic and armour with his sword by his side I imagined him riding out on the crusades to do battle with Moors, and returning home in triumph to claim his lady, as I hoped to do on my trusty Raleigh.

How it all turned out for me remains a secret, but suffice to say that my affection for Broughton remains undiminished through the years!

Enough of boyhood dreams of romance, and on to this church which, because it nestles alongside Sor Brook in the shadow of the castle, has always seemed rather smaller from the outside than it really is.

If it had been situated on the hill overlooking the castle its tower with its octagonal broach spire would have dominated the area, but visitors tend to come across it as an unexpected bonus when visiting the castle.

The historic church of Sir John de Broughton

• *Civil war artefacts found at Broughton Church.*

second 14th century knight, either Sir John's son or grandson.

He wears plate armour of the time of Edward II or Edward III, but I would have no difficulty in placing him as a front row forward in present day England's rugby XV.

I don't know if Banbury School still has 'houses' but when I went to the old County School it had Broughton, Wykham, St Hugh's and Compton (which had the best members by far!) I ought to remember who they were named after - Broughton is obvious, St Hugh was clearly ecclesiastical, and Compton was a knight. Wykham (William) had strong educational links, but I reckon their members would have liked to have been taken to see the effigy of Sir Thomas Wykeham who lies with his wife Elizabeth, and who wears a Yorkist collar of suns and roses, and is dressed in 15th century armour.

Elizabeth was the great niece of William of Wykeham who was Chancellor of England in 1388, and also Bishop of Winchester. Interestingly she wears a Lancastrian collar, so hopefully this was a marriage of peace between the two great houses of the War of the Roses.

It is a bonus because it contains a wealth of 14th century work, although when you look up you can see the original gable ridged roof, and the arcade of four arches which separate the nave from the south aisle, which appear to be mid-12th century. The circular font, with its cable moulding also suggests an earlier 12th century church.

Sir John built the present nave, south aisle and tower, at about the same time as he built his manor house, which Pevsner (have you seen the excellent Saturday night BBC 2 TV series following the great man?) described as 'the most complete mediaeval house in Oxfordshire', and which later became known as the castle.

Accustomed to wooden rood screens in most churches in the area, it is an education to see the fine stone rood screen separating the chancel from the nave, as well carved as any in wood.

But Broughton for me is the church of tombs, for as well as the glorious Sir John, we have a

The Saye and Sele family whose history is intertwined with the church is well represented, and the first Viscount, William Fiennes, was a leading figure in England's second civil war, on the side of the Parliamentarians. He and his wife, Elizabeth lie at the west end of the chancel in altar tombs.

William raised a regiment of blue-coated soldiers who took part in the battle of Edgehill in 1642, but he later opposed the execution of the king, and the dictatorship of the Lord Protector. It was one of the tales I heard as a boy that there was a secret passageway from the Whately Hotel in Horse Fair in Banbury leading to the castle excavated at the time of the Civil War, and together with friends we spent many fruitless hours in the Giant's Cave, with lighted

47

candles looking for some sign of it, as the cave was midway between Banbury and Broughton.

William obviously had enough of wars in England for he later founded Saybrook in Connecticut with Lord Brooke of Warwick who was a partner in the Providence Island Company.

The ten diamond shaped shields on the walls are called hatchments, and range from 1666 to 1847 and they were restored in the United States and returned to the church. All of them commemorate the Fiennes and Twistleton families, whose names are borne by the present Lord Saye and Sele.

The world famous nursery rhyme 'Ride a Cock Horse to Banbury Cross to see a Fyne Lady on a white horse" is now generally said to refer to Celia Fiennes, a diarist who rode a richly caparisoned white horse with tiny tinkling bells - and there is a memorial to Cecile Fiennes in the church which I like to think might have been her.

The church has a clerestory with decorated and perpendicular windows, and the stained

• *The Fiennes family memorial.*

glass is worth a close study. Watch out for the painting of the crucifixion on the pillar behind the font (not easy to see) and the wall paintings which are crying out for restoration. The whole north wall of the Chancel has murals believed to date from the mid 14th century depicting the life and death of the Virgin Mary, who is the patron saint of the church. There is also a fine 15th century brass, and nearby a 13th century decorated stone coffin lid.

Broughton is one of those churches which is steeped in national history, and is well worth a visit. After a walk in the castle grounds a sojourn inside the church reassures the visitor of the permanence of one of the finest parts of England's green and pleasant land.

'Our Lady of Blokesham'
St Mary's Bloxham

Sir John Thorneycroft of Milcombe Hall must have been not only a singularly vain man, but also fairly stubborn and obnoxious. One doesn't like to speak ill of the dead but anyone who has the gall to block up a church window with a marble memorial to his family, despite the objections of the parishioners, and to dig up the ancient burial place of the family whose home he had taken, was hardly likely to win friends and influence people.

However, Sir John did not care, and even boasted in the memorial of coming from an ancient family with 400 years of history in the County Palatine of Chester; and to cap it all he had a figure of himself reclining in full wig at the base.

The memorial is in St Mary's Church, Bloxham, but happily no longer blocks the window, for Victorian architect, G.E.Street, who designed Bloxham College had it moved to its present position in the Milcombe Chapel.

I love churches which pose questions, and 'Our Lady of Blokesham' has so many that it's worth a long visit. It also has some charming and caring members. I met Sarah Carter for instance, who went out of her way to take me home to get the excellent history by Mrs Y.S.Huntriss.

We wondered why Sir John chose to build his memorial at Bloxham rather than Milcombe, but the answer on reflection seems obvious. Bloxham is bigger, finer, and has royal connections, so newcomer Sir John would want to tell everyone just how grand his family was.

Enough of Sir John and back to the questions. Just what is really in the 13th century giant

• The Thorneycroft memorial.

49

painting over the north door which was revealed when the whitewash which the Puritans used to cover it, was removed by Street in 1864? It is supposed to be St Christopher and a mermaid, although if it is a mermaid it would appear to have two tails! Whatever it depicts however one can stand and look at it for a long time and discover all kinds of subjects. This deserves serious restoration.

Above the chancel arch is a spine chilling depiction of the last judgment, and returning to Milcombe Chapel, there is a grand cartoon painting of the life of a young martyr.

Then there is the one solitary fluted or clustered shaft pillar when all the others are just round; why too is there a chevron over the chancel arch window which

is quite out of place with the rest of the carving, and where did the two doorway arches in the clerestory walls lead to?

But that is the charm of Bloxham church. It is so obviously well cared for - John Manning was polishing the brasswork while I was there, and this charming Devonian not only said how much they all liked the Vicar, the Rev John Stroyan, but he pointed out things like the piper with the single chanter in the north wall corner.

Of course recalling the old rhyme - Bloxham for length, Adderbury for strength and King's Sutton for beauty - one has to admire the 198ft spire which towers over the village. Before the present imposing building there was probably a Saxon church because Bloxham was an important manor, and just one year after the Norman conquest the church and manor was granted to Westminster Abbey.

King Stephen endowed a chapel, Henry II gave the patronage to Godstow Abbey which upset Westminster, and in 1547, Edward VI gave the living to Eton College which holds it still.

The Puritans had a big influence, not only covering up the walls, but removing many statues as the empty niches outside show, but the elaborately carved 15th century rood screen, a gift from Cardinal Wolsey after the church was damaged in the Wars of the Roses, survived, and the panels remain unaltered. Other features to look out for are the rare 15th century font, the 14th century priest's room with its fireplace and a window into the church, reached by a spiral staircase; the glorious gargoyles, and the corbels which remind us of Bloxham's royal connections.

Also if you can get hold of the Huntriss guide to the church, do so, if only for gems like this, talking of figures on the cornice outside the north wall of the church - "Here are two men fighting with swords, a whistling man and a man blowing a horn as was usual when approaching a village to announce one's friendly arrival. There are two monkeys riding a cat, two hounds looking at a rabbit in a thicket, a pig with seven piglets, a cock, a fantastic beast and thieving foxes. One is reminded that the fox, in the middle ages, symbolised the devil exercising his wiles to destroy mankind"!

And there's the explanation as to why so many of the carvings in churches round Banbury are similar, for it is believed that in the 14th century there was a talented school of masons at Banbury who travelled round the district.

What that does not explain however is that while on holiday at Tarragona earlier this year I saw carvings, and gargoyles identical to those I had photographed in Adderbury the month before - but then as I said, I love mysteries.

The windows in the church, mainly those in the Milcombe Chapel, give the church much of its light airy appearance. One in the east wall had to be replaced at a cost of £15,000 a few years ago, and it is a great credit to the work that it is almost indistinguishable from the other windows with their mullions and leaded glass.

Elsewhere in the north aisle are the remains of 14th century glass, some stained glass by Morris and Co. of Oxford, and a touching memorial window to Theodore Wood (24), and Gilbert Sutton (26) who both died in 1915 in the 1914-18 war, and to John Sutton who followed his brother only to die in 1918. It shows Sir Galahad, Joan of Arc, and includes the regimental badges of the Royal Artillery, the Dorset regiment and the Oxfordshire and Buckinghamshire Light Infantry.

The Brackley statues which come to life at midnight

IF you stand by St Peter's at Brackley at midnight you may be lucky enough to see the two statues on the tower come to life and step down to quench their thirst at St Rumbold's Well off Water Lane.

However the effigies of St Peter and St Hugh of Lincoln looked pretty immovable to me as they presided benignly from their seats, perhaps enjoying a secret smile about the past beliefs of youngsters of the town.

But it's often youngsters who perpetuate stories and legends of the past, and choirboys, even in comparatively recent times, used to initiate new singers by interring them in the yews that abound in the churchyard.

Whether they knew it or not they were ensuring that the story, first unearthed by the historian John Leland, of the Brackley Vicar who was buried alive 'by the tyranny of a Lord of the towne' did not die.

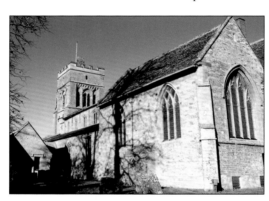

What made it worse was that the Vicar's loyal dog was said to have jumped into the grave to follow his master, so perhaps at midnight he howls to accompany St Hugh and St Peter on their nightly jaunt!

St Peter's, or more correctly St Peter's with St James, which marks the incorporation of St James into the parish in March 1884, now seems an unlikely source for such tales, for with its excellently designed new stone buildings which blend so well with the ancient, it is warm and welcoming.

At first one might think that the outside of the church is more interesting to the visitor, and there's never any doubt about the patron saint, for the superb weather vane with its giant key dominates the tower.

Then there's the ancient sundial set in the wall, so high that you need binoculars, or a telephoto lens to read the legend 'Redeem the time' on it. It was either a bit of a joke to place it as high as it is, or else the Victorians, who carried out a massive restoration, found it elsewhere and stuck it up there out of the way.

There's little doubt that there was a Saxon place of worship on the site for there are some vestigial signs under the present church, but St Peter's was originally a Norman church, with early English and decorated additions from the 13th to the 15th century.

It was lucky that the wife of the vicar, Canon Peter Woodward, and churchwarden Bob Pell (the artist and teacher) were there when I visited, for they kindly showed me the superb Norman doorway with its zigzag carving round the arch which is now in the new building.

It adds a little mystery for it is now in the main church wall, although it was probably part of a porch when the original smaller church was built. Certainly as it is now indoors, it is protected from the elements but the result is that the stonework which has withstood the elements for a thousand years is beginning to flake as it dries out, and the salts from the stone are appearing on the surface like crystalline lichen. However help is on the way for the church is studying ways to preserve this fine reminder of Norman masonry skills.

The church interior is plastered, and the white walls, and the unusual flat, plain ceiling reflects the light from the many stained glass windows.

They are all Victorian but are many and varied, ranging in my view from the very fine to the unremarkable, but you will make up your own minds about that!

All churches have their war memorials and they are always interesting, but St Peter's has one that tells a touching story. There's a window dedicated to Capt Ernest George Campbell of the Rifle Brigade who died of wounds at Bergendall in South Africa on 2nd August 1900, but under the window is a simple but sturdy wooden cross that his widow, Ethel Rosa, brought back from the battlefield in 1903 to put in the church.

There's another touching moment, for a wall mounted monument to Margaret, the eight-year-old daughter of a former Vicar, Henry Manifold, recalls that she died of a 'putrid sore throat' in 1769, and there's a sad obviously deeply felt little quatrain about her.

I love the odd little things you can find if you look hard.

Take this tiny warning on the destruction of churches by fires originating in the organ: "The organ is damp, a lamp or stove is placed on it and left all night with the result of setting it on fire. The Organist, the Blower, the Tuner, or a workman making repairs strikes a match, lights a spirit lamp, taper or a candle which he leaves burning and sets the organ on fire".

It was issued by the Ecclesiastical Insurance Office of the Strand in London, and screwed on to the back of the organ.

No one could miss the way the arcade arches lean outwards however, for they are several degrees out of vertical but, have no fear, they have probably been that way for centuries and the tilt is not getting worse.

Although the Chancel was restored by Lord Francis Egerton in 1837, the three seated sedilia remains, along with the piscina, and there are some beautifully carved miniature masks of St Matthew with wings; St Mark as a lion; St Luke as an ox; and St John as an eagle surmounting the pedestals.

Enjoy the beautifully carved pulpit, which incidentally was on the other side of the chancel arch originally, and the equally impressively carved eagle lectern which was the gift of Charles Dudley in 1803.

Many large vault stones are in the aisles, there's some fine tiling, and there are six bells in the tower. Five were cast by Wells of Leicester in 1628, and a further was added in 1898.

Unusually you enter the church through some fine, tall, light oak tower doors. Again we have another story to explain this – apparently the devil got into the church through the north door, was driven out, and the door was consequently filled in.

It's just like the tale of the two statues – you pays your money and you takes your choice, except that like all the splendid churches in our towns and villages you get the benefit of seeing what are glorious local museums for free, except for a voluntary contribution to the church fabric.

At St Peter's you are also welcomed in, invited to return, and given information about what is clearly a living vibrant church.

Do go and see for yourself – but don't go at midnight, you never know what you might find!

St. Etheldreda, Horley, Oxfordshire

Housewives who have been under pressure during the Festive season could do worse than say a little prayer to St Zita, and if you're one of those people like me who constantly lose your keys, then a candle to the Italian lady might be a good investment!

And if you want to see just what St Zita looked like, visit Horley Church, where near the Norman style 13th century font is a picture of her on one of the pillars.

Zita (1218-72) was a serving maid in Lucca and many miracle stories were told about her. One was that the angels baked her loaves for her while she was 'rapt in ecstasy', and after her death a popular cult grew up around her, with chapels in her honour in places as far afield as Palermo in Sicily and Ely. Her picture also appears in mural paintings in four English counties, where she was known as St Sithes.

In the Middle Ages her aid was invoked by housewives, and domestic servants, especially when they had lost their keys, or were in danger from crossing bridges or

• *The painting of St Christopher and (right) the famous Horley fishermen - the earliest known depiction.*

rivers - I wonder if it would work for the Channel Tunnel?

Horley is distinctive in that it has a central tower, and three interesting Early English doors, but its real glories are the wall paintings, dominated by the huge St Christopher on the north aisle wall, painted in 1450.

One of the things that has become more and more apparent when looking at local churches has been to imagine what effect such paintings must have had on the

• *The medallions with the repeated letter 'T' which may relate to Thomas a Beckett and the picture of St Zita.*

village inhabitants. In days when most of us lived in grass covered huts without any kind of pictures, no music, and no architecture, to step into a church like St Etheldreda's at Horley and see brilliant murals, and hear plainsong, must have been like seeing TV for the first time, or going to the theatre.

Joan Bowes, who now lives at Chacombe, says this about the St Christopher: "Hopefully you looked at this first on entering the church, so you are now according to tradition, saved from sudden death today! St Christopher was a giant who was flayed and burned alive for his Christian faith. He carried the Christ-child and in astonishment at his weight, asked 'What art though so yonge, bar I never so hevy a thinge' The reply was 'Yey, I be hevy no wonder ys for I am ye Kinge of Blys'". The picture is fascinating because it contains the earliest known pictures of anglers with rod and line in England, and even more fascinating because the fish seem to be sturgeon - hardly

likely to be found in the Sor Brook or the Cherwell even in those unpolluted days. It may be, however, that the artist drew them from dried sea fish specimens imported by local monks or clergy who would have appreciated this fine game fish!

St Etheldreda was born about 630AD in Exning in W.Suffolk, and she was the daughter of the first Christian king of East Anglia. After two unconsummated marriages she became a nun in Northumberland, and later founded a double monastery at Ely. There are only 12 churches dedicated to her in England, and nine of these are in the eastern counties. The dedication leads to the suspicion that there was a Saxon church at Horley before the tower was built in 1100, and Queen Edith, the wife of Edward the Confessor held the manorial rights to both Horley and Hornton. There are Saxon stones, and one bearing a cross by the south door.

Inside the church, the lines of the early

pitched roof can be seen above the brightly painted and highly decorative reconstructed rood loft and screen with its lifelike figures. It dominates the church along with St Christopher but it does tend to hide the original chancel arch.

By the arch are a series of medallions with the letter T repeated which may relate to Thomas a Beckett of Canterbury, killed in 1170AD by King Henry's three knights.

Joan Bowes thinks the village could have been engaged in St Thomassing or 'trick-a-treating', a North Oxfordshire pastime before Christmas in the past, and now a custom returned from N.America to Britain at Hallowe'en.

The church was a useful training ground for top ecclesiastics for in the 15th century Henry Romwarth of Horley became Archdeacon at Canterbury, Robertus Gylbard was later Bishop of London, and a century later, Robert Pate was Chaplain to Henry VIII.

For those readers who like brasses, there is a fine 15th century plate on the floor of the church tower which shows a husband and wife, several sons and six daughters!

While the main body of the church feels, and is, clearly mediaeval, the chancel, cut off by the tower with its half arches within (one with stone coffin), seems austerely plain. It does have a beautifully carved Norman piscina by the altar, and the Creed and the Ten Commandments carved on black marble on the

• *The highly decorated font at St Etheldredas.*

white walls.

There are plenty of things to see in this Hornton stone church, including the domestic chamber organ built in 1765, the sturdy and self important Victorian coke burning furnace surmounted by a crown by the Gurney Central Heating Company, and the 1713 chest.

Outside are some impressive 18th century memorials on the church walls, and a fine sundial on the west corner, which was restored in memory of John Saunders, the professional photographer whose work we have reproduced in Banbury Fare, and who was a regular contributor to Country Life, providing many a front cover for the magazine.

While Horley has a history stretching back to Saxon times, it has had its problems. In 1621 it was reported to be 'ruinous and decayed' and by 1632 'ready to fall'. Since then it has undergone rebuilding in every century until in 1950 it had several fine restorations under the will of John Clement Ansell of Horley Manor and carried out by architect, Lawrence Dale.

Dominating Deddington Ridge - St Peter and Paul

I found the squirrel at Deddington Church, and it wasn't easy! Indeed without the excellent short guide (great value at 20p) which gave me the hint that it was on the right hand side of the heavy west door, I would still be looking - as I am still looking for the cat and the green man on the side of the kneeling desk. They are all carvings and just part of the attraction of this great church.

However, it is just a shadow of its former self, as indeed is the village. For at one time Deddington was far more important than Banbury, with its own castle (sadly now just a grassy mound) and with fine houses - many of which thankfully, are still there.

The present church with its tower and its eight golden weather

vanes dominates the Deddington ridge, and can be seen for many miles, but when the original 13th century church was built it had a spire, and that must have been an even more impressive landmark. It's a fair bet that with the great spires of Adderbury, Bloxham and King's Sutton well within view, Deddington 's spire would have to have been something special as befitted the church of a town at an important cross-roads.

Unfortunately however, in March 1634 the tall steeple and bell tower collapsed into the body of the church and did immense damage, and the church was unusable for several years. Rather like St Mary's at Banbury, the original church must have been a very fine building with two floors, and several chapels until the Reformation, and the upper row of six windows that still remain provided the light for them.

But enough of the church that was - what about the church that is.

First impression as you enter by the south door is that here is a much loved church, for on the first warm morning in October, the masses of flowers which decorate it were caught in the sunlight streaming in from the plain mullioned glass windows.

which has some 15th century workmanship - the eye is at once caught by ten wooden crosses on the wall which were brought to England from the 1914-18 war. They were on the graves of Deddington soldiers, who

What made it more fun was that a score or so people had arrived for the Friday coffee were re-interred by the Commonwealth War Grave Commission and one is particularly

morning for the Katharine House Hospice, organised by Pat Brittain. With a kitchen and toilet block in light oak just inside the door, this is a church designed to be used.

The genial bearded Vicar, the Rev Ken Reeves, showed me the four decorated sedilia (Priest's seats) in the chancel which are probably the oldest part of the

touching, for it is dated November lst 1918, just ten days before the end of the war.

There are two piscina, an interesting effigy of a local 14th century lawyer, Ralph de Beriford (Barford) in a recess in the south wall, but by far the most impressive is the fan tracery in the domed roof of the north porch, but you might be advised to

church. The 13th century font was destroyed in the great fall, and the present one is mid-Victorian with a splendid wooden cover - which also has a squirrel on it, but I did not find that one.

Looking straight across this mainly square church - the chancel is rather like an addition separated by the fine rood screen

take a torch to see the full beauty of this.

In many places there are half arches that disappear, hints of stone stairways, evidence of a lower level of use, and there was once a Priest's room over the south porch - as at Bloxham church.

There are few really old memorials, but several to the Churchill family and to the

Stilgoes, and just three faces in the roof by the north wall.

The windows are the subject of a fine pamphlet by Elizabeth Tuthill, and she details the 'predominance of blue and green tinted glass' with 'an extraordinary feeling of tranquillity and prayerfulness' in the Emily May Jones memorial window. The Muriel Vane Jones window is remarkable for its strong 1930's feel with the children and even the angel in 1930's style.

Enjoy the windows, the stone tomb chest, the late 14th century brass of the upper part of a bearded man of Edward III's reign and the list of Rectors and Vicars of the church - the first being Ranulph Brito le Bret who died in 1247.

The church itself has wide aisles, grand dimensions, and thankfully, now a firm feeling of solidity, thanks to Charles I who ordered its rebuilding.

Although it is large and spacious, it was not big enough for its hey day in the early 19th century, when a gallery was put up at the west end to seat more people, one of whom was Oxford student John Henry Newman, later Cardinal Newman.

Another famous man who almost certainly worshipped at the church in 1312 was the Gascon knight, the Earl of Cornwall, Piers Gaveston, who was the homosexual favourite of King Edward II. He lodged at the nearby Rectory and was taken to Warwick Castle by the Earls of

• *This Norman knight can be found in the tower recess, while at the top of the column is the crest of the Humphrey-Pargeter family.*

Lancaster and Warwick. From there he was marched barefoot to Blacklow Hill and beheaded.

Gaveston is commemorated in the Grant of Arms to Deddington in the form of a chained eagle.

More savoury is the memorial in the church to the Harris family which has three hedgehogs on the crest, for Mr Harris was a Deddington butcher who was famed for his sausages and pies!

Following in the drovers' footsteps

IF you go to the Three Conies at Thorpe Mandeville for a meal, and then wander through the village towards Culworth, pop in to the 14th century church of St John the Baptist.

If you do, you will be following an ancient tradition. First you will have eaten at a hostelry which gave shelter in the 17th century, and probably much earlier than that, to the drovers who herded sheep and cattle along what was formerly Banbury Lane. Then you will pause to pray for good fortune, as they did on their journey south in what was originally a Saxon holy place, and probably before that a grove that was sacred to the Druids.

For in the churchyard close to the church is a yew tree, which at the base is more than seven yards in circumference, that was certified in March 1989 to be at least 1,000 years old by the Yew Tree Campaign, and trees played a vital role in Druid worship.

It was likely that the Saxon Christians took over from the Druids, and they in turn were replaced by the Normans, with the village taking its name Thorpe from the Saxon for a village, and Mandeville from a Norman family, probably corrupted from Main de Ville, or holder of the town.

Whatever your reason, you can be sure that the church will repay your interest. The porch has a king and queen to welcome you, and a carved stone arch which is known as a crocketted ogee dripstone!

Enter the church and you will see the three double chamfered arches, but look left to the base of the tower with its pretty recessed lancet window. Go into the tower and there's a splendid monochrome full length painting on metal of a mediaeval knight and his lady.

Turn the corner outside the tower and prepare to be amazed by the stone 16th century Kirton memorial to Thomas, a Common Serjeant of the City of London, his wife Mary, and their 12 children, six sons and six daughters. They are all dressed in late Tudor style, and the work is detailed and informative.

Anyone who likes visiting our churches will appreciate good workmanship and there is a fine bier which was made in 1922 and given by Thomas Goffe 'in pleasant memories of this place'.

Just who was King Sigebert? I ask because he is featured in one of the three beautiful stained glass windows dedicated to

• *This Norman knight can be found in the tower recess.*

61

the memory of William Thomas Browning by his pupils. Of course King Henry VI, King Alfred, and William of Wykeham are well known, and I've heard the names of Thomas Sutton of Charterhouse, and Laurence Sheriff – but Sigebert, he remains a mystery.

If you are serious about really seeing what treasures linger in our churches, it's vital to take a high powered torch. If you do, you will be able to see the fine murals on the north wall, where Jesus sits on Saint Christopher's shoulders.

No doubt the drovers would have appreciated seeing the patron saint of travellers depicted, and one imagines would have offered a gift or two in return for a blessing on both them and their animals.

Humphrey is a name that dominates the many wall memorials in the church, and like all families in the second decade of the 20th century suffered great loss in the 1914-18 war. Capt Albert Humphrey MC of the 23rd Royal Fusiliers, and Lt Douglas Humphrey of the 2nd Oxford and Bucks LI were both casualties. Along with the names of others who fell they are recorded on a beautifully carved wooden plaque.

The Humphreys had some remarkable names. One was Natheniel, another was Nathanael, and yet a third was named Nathaniel. Nathanael had a wife called Kezia, and other Humphreys rejoiced in the names of Ptolomey, and Raphael. The family was linked with the Pargeters, and their combined coats of arms may be seen on memorials in the chancel. The Humphreys were gifted people, Raphael was a member of the Inner Temple in London, and recently, Stuart was an Ophthalmic Surgeon. No fewer than five Rectors came from the family between 1727 and 1902.

Most of the memorials are in the chancel, and another one records the Rev Henry William Pullen, who was Rector, and also Chaplain to Her Majesty's Arctic Expedition in 1875-6. Nearby is an iron or bronze depiction of the Last Supper, and again a torch is a useful asset here, and alongside is a half size St Nicholas on the wall painted in a similar fashion to a Russian ikon.

Which brings us to the carved wooden altar which also has circular Russian inlaid paintings of the four New Testament writers, St Matthew, St Mark, St Luke and St John, and this

• *The windows dedicated to William Browning.* **Upper**: *William of Wykeham, and King Henry VI.* **Middle**: *Laurence Sheriff and Thomas Sutton.* **Lower**: *King Alfred and King Sigebert.*

brings an exotic touch to what is predominantly a simple building.

Another unusual name is that of Dorothy Barlee, who was the daughter of John Barlee, described as a Citizen of London. She died in 1714 and there is a memorial to her in the chancel. It's always surprising in the days of bone rattling coach travel to find so many links with the nation's capital in our village churches.

I'm always fascinated by the piscinas, the stone basins for hand washing, and by aumbreys for the everlasting light, and while St John's has a piscina, it also has an aumlrey for the sacred vessels for the altar, although they also served another purpose, to hold gifts for the poor.

A reminder of a disease that haunted the Middle Ages, and which the climate change doom mongers say may return to England, is the little leper's window in the chancel, through which food and drink could be pushed out for the sufferers outside the church.

I know that some readers like to know about

• *A spectacularly beautiful crest in the window by the pulpit on the south wall.*

church organs and the one at St John's was made by Nicholson of Worcester, and the electric blower was given in memory of Mary Annie Webb.

Church bells also cast their own spell, and once again we see the name Bagley of Chacombe. No 2 bell is inscribed: 'Henry Bagle (sic) made mee 1636, God Save King Charles'. The other two bells were made in 1790 (in Hertford) and 1827 (in Oxford).

Outside, the churchyard is very well kept, and the church itself is unusual in that the tower is quite distinctive with its small roofed gable, which Maurice Cole, the author of an informative pamphlet in the church, and also of a book called 'The History of Thorpe Mandeville' (obtainable on 01295 711042) describes as 'a pack saddle steeple' an early tower covering.

We know our readers tend to keep past issues of the magazine so some will recall the tombstone to the black slave at Culworth church. Apparently black youngsters, both slaves and servants were not uncommon in the big houses around Banbury, for the church registers show that 'Richard, a black boy, aged nine years born in the East Indies, 28th July, 1751' was baptised in the church, just a few miles from Culworth.

The church itself is probably 14th century although there was a church building in 1163 linked to a convent at Daventry. The walls inside show the marks of a pitched roof very similar to a large Saxon barn.

Now the really good time to visit the church must be at Easter.

I say this because even at the end of a cold February, there were some superb spring flowers ornamenting the pulpit and other parts of the church, a marvellous welcome to any visitor and a fine adornment to an equally fine building.

Whoever had provided this burst of colour is a talented flower arranger and the church is lucky to have their services.

• *The 13th century church of St John the Baptist at Thorpe Mandeville which stands on the site of a much earlier place of worship.*

Is there something in the water at Aston Le Walls?

VOLVIC – that's the name of a brand of bottled water currently being advertised on TV which claims it comes from a volcanic area in France where the men and women are reputed to be very keen on making whoopee, as the 1930s American song had it, thanks to drinking the beverage.

Now there's no record of Aston le Walls being in a volcanic area, but there's ample evidence that in the past the ladies were exceptionally fertile, and the men obviously no slouches in that department either!

How do we know? Because in the 13th century church of St Leonard's there is a brass now on the south wall, but once on the floor, which commemorates Albanus Butler who was the Lord of the Manor of Ashton (sic) le Walls, whose wife had no fewer than five sons and seven daughters, and alongside another to his son, George, who had ten sons and three daughters!

Of these eight remained, John, George, Simon, Robert, Ambrose, Samuel, Elizabeth and Martha. We have no record of how fecund they were, but the Butlers of Bloxham, who are keen on family records may know of some connection.

Albanus Butler, who was married to Sybil, daughter of Rawleigh de Thornborowe in Warwickshire died in 1609, and George Butler died in 1685.

Only three years later, the Rector John Wilson also passed away and his wife Sarah King, bore him five sons and six daughters, so certainly in the 18th century there must have been something in the water at Ashton le Walls, as it was known at the time.

It is something of a surprise to come across such a good church as St Leonard's in a comparatively small village but at one time it was clearly an important building.

Although the chancel was built some time after the nave, it has three seats for priests, and room for five – and it has two piscinae for washing the Communion vessels, in the north wall. This suggests that with provision for that number of clergy the services must have been quite something.

Also in the chancel is a fine tomb of a young cleric, and the stone arched recess in which he rests adjoins the aumbrey door, which has some fine ironwork that has survived for at least 600 years.

The chancel like the rest of the church was extensively restored in the last years of the 19th and in the early 20th century,

and that has given it a superb marble and basalt reredos at the back of the altar, and a particularly fine tiled floor. The oak choir stalls are also beautifully carved, sturdy and richly coloured and polished.

The nave floor is untiled, but has the original stone, along with various large tombstones mostly hidden by the carpets, but they are moveable and reveal some interesting details.

The plain pillars in the nave are Norman, along with the square font which has a well preserved carving of the tree of life and the real feel of antiquity. Also Norman is the arch in the tower which is a very good example of the architecture of the period.

All the stonework in the church has been very well restored, and looks as if it has

only recently been erected – and that really is amazing in a building of this age.

The tower must have been repaired and partially rebuilt after 1907 because there is a photograph on the south wall which shows a sizeable part of it falling down with a great hole in the side. Was it struck by lightning one wonders?

Another eye-catcher is the organ with its green, red and gold pipes. Sadly I could not find anything to tell us who made it, but it really is quite a fine instrument, and it's a shame it is somewhat hidden behind the arch nearest to the chancel in the north aisle.

There's a good looking clock on the tower, but once again I have to confess I could find nothing about the bells,

although the clock has a muffled chime as it thumps, rather than rings out the hours.

Looking upwards the nave has a 15th century wooden roof which was covered in aluminium in 1946, and the chancel has a Victorian/Edwardian roof with

good timbers. In the nave there remain some fine stone heads at the base of the roof timbers, but little else remains of any decorative sculpture.

No stained glass in this church but plenty of light through the diamond green, pink and pale blue mullioned windows

There are three church chests, all of varying age, and a pulpit and lectern which match the fine pews.

There are a few memorials, but the largest on the east wall adjoining the nave is the most interesting.

It reads: "Let no man rase this Remembrance nor disturb the dust of Mrs Eliz wife of Tho Orme of Hanch Hall, by Lichfield in Com. Staff Esq. Daughter of and Cohr of Wm Marshall of Yorkshire G. She at 7 could read distinctly to the Sence and at 13 had finished works like a Curious Needlewoman. Her riper years past in frequent reading Divinity observing ye Discipline of ye Church of England. Could I insert her unaffected dressing, her neat body, her Decorum in Housekeeping, her Charity etc. A larger table could not contain it. She languished long with difficulties to very many Physicians and artists. On ye 20th of Jan 1692 her breath expired Having pray'd many days incessantly"

We have kept the capitals and abbreviations etc as they are on the inscription, and one can only think the mason charged his fee by the letter and was advised to condense the names. Surprisingly too, the actual inscription did not quite fit in the space left for it and the last three lines are on a separate plaque below, although in the same stone.

In the stone floor by the organ is a crest, now indecipherable, although the name Rathbone can be seen nearby and the initials TB.

In the south wall is a memorial to the Berdmore family – Ann (d.1753), Edward (d.1769), Thomas (the Rector, who died in 1774) and Sarah (d.1786). The memorial was erected by their sister Sarah Stopes in 1792. There's also a memorial to another Rector, Richard Webster, who died in 1851 aged 78, after 36 years serving the village.

Outside the church there is a small Tudor building tacked on the tower which once served as a porch and on the west side of the nave there is an empty arched tomb recess. Not far away is a perfectly round stone about seven inches high and a foot and a half across which may have been the base of a preaching cross.

Wander round to the north side and there is an ancient blocked up door with a chimney that one presumes once served the boiler for the long defunct under floor heating.

Those readers who enjoy tombstones will find a plethora of 18th century memorials, and a few earlier than that, and there are many ornate chest tombs, and one coffin tomb. There are some massive memorial slabs to the Mattingley family which must have flourished in the 19th century.

A hefty yew tree marks the path leading to the church, dominating the well kept churchyard.

But back inside the church there are three other important memorials – but of quite a different kind. The church has no fewer than three beautifully leather bound books of Common Prayer.

The oldest dates from 1731. Printed by the "Assigns of His Majesty's Printer, and of Henry Hills deceased". It cost just eight shillings (40p) and was 'The gift of Mr Knightly Wilson, the Rector, to the Parish Church of Aston le Walls. December 9th 1733.

The next in date was printed in 1790 at Oxford, by W.Jackson and A.Hamilton, printers to the University. This has the date 1796 inscribed in gold on red leather.

By 1800 the price of the book of Common Prayer had risen to 17s (85p) – so inflation is not a new phenomenon – and this one was again printed at Oxford, this time by Bensley and Cooke, also printers to the University.

Coming more up-to-date is the fine bible, printed in Glasgow in 1862 and this was given in memory of Wallace Cooknell (1911 - 1978).

And, slap bang up-to-date right into the 21st century, is the bible presented by George and Lil Goodman (1992-2002) 'in appreciation for the warmth, kindness and friendship given to us by parishioners during our happy years at Cherry Tree Cottage'.

It's good to think that hopefully this latest gift will exercise the same fascination for future generations as the 1733 Book of Common Prayer has for us today.

When Banbury saved Byfield's Puritans

ONE of the worst things about our modern villages from the aesthetic point of view – especially in Northamptonshire – is the preponderance of overhead cables.

In Byfield for instance, it is almost impossible to get an uncluttered picture of the church of the Holy Cross, which was originally dedicated to St Helena. Consequently I make no apology for the leaning verticals in the picture because they were sacrificed to avoid the thick electricity cables.

However the sheer quality of the church architecture remains, especially the fine windows, and the tower which has had the spire added to the battlements of the original.

The battlements would have been a bit late to defend the village of Bivivella, for in 917 a Danish army roared out from Northampton into the Banbury area and killed many people, especially in one battle at Hook Norton.

Then in 1010 the Northumbrians came south to this part of Northamptonshire to kill, burn and take many captives.

By the time of the Domesday Book in 1087 there was a church in the village, for Robert de Rothelent, gave with Hugh, Earl of Chester's consent, the church to the abbey of St Ebrulf at Utica in Normandy, which had a priory at Ware in Hertfordshire.

When we have problems with the French we tend to stop buying their soggy apples, or their rather more palatable cheeses. But in 1414 in The Hundred Year war against France, King Henry V decided to expel all the foreign religious members and kept their possessions for himself, so Byfield church went to the Carthusian monastery of Jesus of Bethlehem in Surrey.

What goes around comes

around as they say, and in the 16th century King Henry VIII dispossessed the monasteries, and Sir Richard Knightley of Fawsley became the patron, and members of his family were Rectors over the next 200 years. Finally the patronage was acquired by Corpus Christi College, Oxford.

The present church dates from around 1340 and was dedicated to St Helena, mother of the Roman Emperor, Constantine. She was reputed to have discovered the actual cross on which Christ was crucified, and she was also mistakenly believed to have been English.

The first actual Rector of the church – the present one is a lady, the Rev Lynda Randall – was John of Exon, who was later Chancellor of York, and then Bishop of Winchester. He supported Simon de Montfort against Henry III and for that he was retired to Rome. Lynda also looks after Boddington and Aston le Walls.

Anyone who is watching the current series 'The History of Britain' on BBC 2, will have seen how apocalyptic the Black Death was for Britain, with half the population dying from the rat born disease. Byfield's present church was built just a year before the plague struck so its Decorated style must have been some comfort for the remaining villagers. It has a chancel, clerestoried nave of four bays, aisles, a south lady chapel, and a south porch.

Pevsner called the building 'ambitious' and he liked the ball flower decoration of the porch.

There's no rood screen for the chancel, but at one time it had several altars, a high altar, and one, of course, was dedicated to St Helen.

In the early 17th century the church was described as having no stairs for its pulpit, and then described as wanting a decent pulpit. Now it has a surfeit of pulpits! It has the one in use which appears Jacobean, and a gloriously decorated one at the back of the church which came from Corpus Christi at Oxford, and proved far too heavy for the existing support. It's well worth a look.

Lecterns seldom get a mention, but I recall the brass eagle at Cropredy with its slot for St Peter's pence. However, I have yet to see one more interesting than the exquisitely carved wooden example at Byfield. It has four miniature figures at the base, each of which is a work of art on its own account.

Sadly, although there is a first class history of Byfield and the church, there is no reference to when the lectern was made or who the talented carpenter was.

The church has plain walls, but once surely must have had murals; its pillars are strong but unadorned, and the stained glass windows are Victorian, with the impressive east window by Kempe.

There were however two stained glass mediaeval roundels which have been loaned to Ely Stained Glass Museum. The first depicts a hind seated on a mound covered with grass and flowers. The hind was the insignia of Queen Philippa of Hainault, wife of Edward III, and was a familiar Yorkist propaganda device in the Wars of the Roses.

The second shows a fox in priest's clothing in a pulpit preaching to a flock of geese, and the fox has grabbed one unsuspecting goose by the throat. There's a similar one in Leicester Cathedral, and shows there was some cynicism about some of the clergy at that time, and also a good sense of humour on the part of the designer!

When you visit the church you will immediately see four massive stone gargoyles, which were removed from the tower in 1952. Normally seeing the gargoyles in situ on the outside of the church one remarks on their design and passes on. But seen up close their sheer hideousness is impressive, although their practical use as waterspouts is obvious.

Once more our old friend, Bagley, the bell-founder from Chacombe has turned up again. The fourth bell at Byfield has the inscription:

"Be it known to all who doe me see

That Wm Bagley of Chalcombe(sic) made mee".

William also made the second and third bells in the early 19th century. However, bells have rung out over the village since 1552.

Regular readers will recall that there is a fine matchstick model of 'the Feldon Cathedral' at Brailes church, and there's an equally fine model (although smaller and not constructed from matchsticks) at Byfield, made by Miss Agnes Fairbrother in 1886.

Piscinas and sedilia are worth looking at, as is the particularly fine alabaster reredos,

plus the differing carved wooden pew ends. In the 1870s when so much restoration took place in local churches, two stone crosses were unearthed and they are now on the north wall of the church. The leper window in the chancel was also rediscovered, plus the remains of some ancient coffins. There are two wall memorials in the chancel, and some interesting carved memorials in the stone floor, also in the chancel.

Apart from the stained glass there are some clear leaded windows, and one was restored thanks to a bequest by Raymond Phizacklea, former Head Teacher of Byfield School, who died in Canada, aged 51, in 1979.

There's plenty of modern evidence that the church is well cared for and caters for all ages, and while not as ostentatious as some seen recently, it has a singular attraction all of its own. However, one suspects that its simplicity hides a remarkable history in a village which has links with the Wars of the Roses, the Lollards, and the Civil War.

In the latter, Byfield remained loyal to the king, with dire consequences for visiting Puritans.

Parliamentary troops arriving at Byfield in the beginning of the war were not well received and one wrote: 'we could get no quarter, neither meat, drink or lodgings and had we not been supplied with ten cartloads of provisions and beer from Banbury many of us would have perished'.

Good for Banbury!

69

Warwickshire's 'Feldon' cathedral watched over by swallows

My family have nested in the church porch for over 20 years. We do ask that human visitors are considerate and also give notice that we can take no responsibility for anyone tripping over our box. Thank you'. From the Swallows!

That is the charming notice that greets anyone pausing to look into St George's Church at Brailes as they negotiate the sizeable cardboard tray placed to avoid the swallows' droppings landing on the stone floor from the nests above.

However, I guarantee that anyone who does stop at the church will do a great deal more than pause, for there is almost an embarrassment of riches for aficionados of our beautiful village churches.

But to call St George's 'a village church' is to do it less than justice, for not for nothing is it called 'the Cathedral of the Feldon'. Feldon? That is the name for the countryside or 'fieldland' south of the River Avon, and 'Cathedral' is not too grandiose, considering the history of Brailes.

For Brailes in the mid 16th century was a 'parish of great compass' with '2000 houselying people'

which made it the largest town in Warwickshire after Coventry and Warwick, at a time when Birmingham was only a hamlet. Its church which is 162ft long, by 57ft wide, with a 110ft tower befits its status at the time, and today is still a stunningly impressive building.

It probably began life in Saxon times, as a few stones in the tower testify, and the first incumbent is recorded as Geoffrey in 1153. The church as we see it dates mainly from the early 14th century in the Decorated style, when Brailes was a bustling market town with a water mill and an important wool trade. Just as the church was beginning to take shape however, the Black Death struck in 1349 and disrupted building, to be followed by the plague in 1360, which probably claimed the then incumbent Robert Mile, who was succeeded in 1361 by William of Bradway.

Brailes seems to have been singularly unlucky for there was another plague in 1603 which lasted a year, and more recently in 1876 there was another disaster, for a diamond tiled plaque in the west wall touchingly records that the window above was in memory of the 37 dear children who died in this parish of diphtheria. Dedicated by their teachers and friends".

Of course, churches are the place for memorials, but I particularly like this one to Richard Davies, a Master of Arts at Exeter College, Oxford, who died aged 36 in 1639. After a eulogy there is this splendid verse:

> "Though dead hee bee, yet lives his fame
>   Like rose in June so smells his name
>   Rejoyce wee at his change, not faint
>   Death kil'd a man but made a saint".

Much more modern and amazingly translucent, is an example of modern stained glass that in the right light sparkles and shimmers. It is in the north wall and is dedicated to Douglas William Cummings, who was a churchwarden and chorister and who died in 1993.

This window is outstanding, although it is much smaller than the superb windows at both the east and west ends which are set off by the soaring broad arches which justify the 'Cathedral' description; even smaller still are the Flemish medallions reset in the south windows this year, which date from the 16th century.

On the afternoon I visited, I was lucky to meet the Vicar, the Rev Nicholas Morgan, not only because he is a man who clearly loves his church, but because

he pointed out the Brailes Icon – a particularly fine wood carving executed in 1998 by sculptor Nadin Senft, which because of the strong sunlight behind it was only a silhouette until I studied it further. If you visit in the afternoon be sure to buy a postcard of this piece if you are at all artistic.

While on the subject of postcards, and publications don't miss the composite postcard of the church, which is from photographs taken by the Vicar, who

coincidentally uses a much underrated Yashica Electro GT camera, bought by him at an auction for church funds. This is the same model as the one once used by me, and now by the *Four Shires'* publisher for some of the pictures in the magazine.

The Vicar also produced the historical notes on the church, which are a 'must' for any visitors, and remarkably inexpensive, although that does not stop you paying more!

Although I am loth to disagree with a learned cleric, I have to say that the tomb chest which has a much weathered recumbent figure in limestone leads me to agree with a local tradition that it is of an unknown crusader, if only for the little dog at his feet. However it has been dated at about 1450 and could be that of Robert Bandy, Vicar in 1433-1455. We will never know.

I loved the story he told me about the 1650 oak chest which has the date 1758 BC inscribed on its lid.

"I was showing it to some American visitors one day" said the Vicar "as an example of something ancient in the church. They were suitably impressed and said 'Gee, is it really as old as that' firmly believing that the BC was an historical date, rather than standing for Brailes Church!".

I spoke about the embarrassment of riches, and one of the most remarkable is the matchstick model of the church which was completed in 1979, and which used 250,000 matchsticks, and took seven years to complete. It was made by Fred Hall of Shipston on Stour, and it was

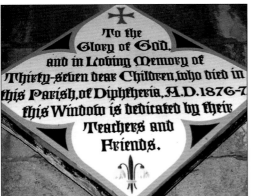

• *The fine glass at Brailes church includes depictions of The Crucifixion (over right) and a 17th century Palm Sunday (left). Pictured above is the 1540 depiction of the boy Jesus in the temple. The memorial window to Douglas William Cummings shows that modern stained glass is as fine as any of the past. Pictured bottom left is the sad memorial to 37 young victims of diphtheria.*

his wish that it should be used to raise funds for the upkeep of the church.

Undoubtedly, the star of the show however, is the Millennium Altar Frontal designed and made by Alison Binns who used silk with a variety of applied fabrics and leather with silk paint. The techniques she used are applique, quilting and stumpwork with a variety of stitching. Once again there is a fully explanatory publication about how the work was done and what it signifies, and anyone who appreciates real craftsmanship and symbolism will simply love it.

Only a few feet away from the altar are three fine sedilia (seats) with two exquisite carved heads, and in the centre of the church is an excellent covered octagonal 14th century font, deep enough to completely immerse an infant. Each of the eight faces which at a glance look the same, has a slightly different design.

We looked at Warmington's fine mobile Millennium screen, but we have to say it would be dwarfed by the tapestry screen on the fine light oak panel at the entrance to the Brailes tower, for it has more than 160 squares depicting village life and it was dedicated on St George's Day, 1990. It took three years hard work by Brailes' villagers, and was a feature of BBC's Songs of Praise broadcast some years ago.

Other things to see are the wicker work Bath chair, the internal clock mechanism on display, the 1812 Parish hand bell, the stone seat outside the porch which has been worn into a comfortable shape by countless bottoms, and the vast number of gravestones.

There must be a story about the imposing tomb surmounted by two copper sphinxes dedicated to Alicia Sheldon, daughter of General Sir Evan Lloyd, who died in March 1896, for it was erected by Isabel Calmady 'the last of the Sheldons'.

It must be worth some research, as would be the tombstone in the chancel to Mary Bishop, who died aged just 25 in 1724, which has an armorial crest on it.

Brailes had its share of benefactors, and they are recorded on plaques around the walls. For instance, James Cooper of Clerkenwell left £100 in 1678 for cloth for the poor people of the village, and Francis Capell in 1704 left £10 for the 15 poorest Protestant widows, plus two gowns and five shillings' (25p) worth of bread for regular distribution.

I haven't touched on the six bells, but 'Merry George' was recast in 1671 and has the rhyme: "I'll crack no more so ring your fill, Merry George I was and will be still" while the fourth bell was also recast in 1688 and 1900 and has this inscription: "I'm not the bell I was but quite another. I'm now as rite and sweet as George, my brother".

Together, the six bells are reputed to be the second heaviest of six in England. There's still more to see, so allow yourself plenty of time to enjoy this 'cathedral'. I guarantee that if you do you will see why Vicar Nicholas Morgan says: "We are very proud of our Parish Church, perhaps the grandest in Warwickshire".

73

'O hurrying traveller grudge not to check thy steps and ponder well' at St James, Somerton

I DON'T suppose there could be anything more English than the evocative smell of newly mown grass in a churchyard on a sun-drenched early spring day and from the moment that I saw the tower of St James at Somerton I knew I was in for a treat.

And with that vision of the walls with their battlements came the certainty that although Somerton is now a comparatively small village by Oxfordshire standards, at one time it must have been important, commanding as it does a crossing in the Cherwell flood plain.

Only a glance inside through the amazingly ancient outer north door confirmed that view. This is a church of character and importance, and its splendid 15th century chancel screen and three north arcades, plus its 12th century north aisle would make it impressive enough for anyone.

However on the south side behind another panelled screen lies real treasure. The south chapel which was enlarged in the 17th century from the original 14th century south aisle,

retains two arches from that time and contains three splendid marble tombs to the Fermor family. It also has several wall plaques and three hatchments, and two fine brasses along with a floor made almost entirely of memorial stones.

Almost, because if you enter the chapel from the chancel you will be walking on a segment of what looks like the original small 14th century tiles.

You will pass the organ which surprisingly is in the chapel rather than the chancel. Sadly there are no details about the instrument except that it was hand blown and still has the wooden lever, although it was converted to an electric blower by Mr and Mrs Hill of Troy, Somerton, in memory of Antony 1934-1953.

Immediately in front you will see the massive chest tomb to Thomas Fermor and his wife, Brigitta. Their effigies lie on top and they are dressed in their Tudor garments and armour, and the inscription reads: " To Thomas Fermor Esq, Knight, a man of (the dots signify some illegible carving)

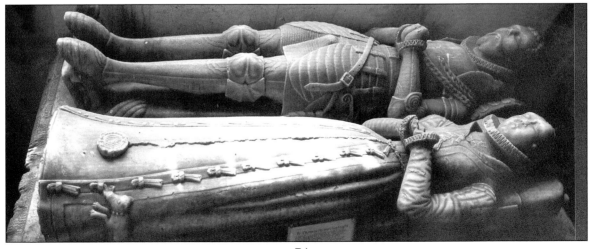

generosity towards scholars, mercy and goodness towards his people, admirable piety to all men, the kindly lord of this estate and the excellent founder of a school in perpetual memory of himself and his beloved wife, Brigitta, his executors in accordance with his wishes, have with tears erected this monument. He died in the year of our Lord 1580".

The Fermors acquired the manor of Somerton in 1512, and Thomas was Lord of the Manor from 1552 until his death. He remained a Roman Catholic throughout his life and endowed the village school which survived for nearly 400 years!

Nearby against the south wall is the tomb of Richard Fermor, Thomas's son who died in 1642 and his epitaph reads: " You ask who I am that lies beneath marble. Once I was Richard Fermor. Part of me remains, ashes to ashes, part scales the heights of heaven. That thou mayest act thus in death, in life act likewise".

Opposite backing on to the nave lies the ornate tomb of John Fermor, eldest son of Richard, and inscribed there is this fine exhortation –

"O hurrying traveller grudge not to check thy steps; see who I was and ponder well. My name was John Fermor, the eldest son of his parents and the first hope of the family of the House of Fermor. I was in the flower of youth, my cheeks were bright and blooming, and having just married my wife I was full of joy. Scarcely had I begun my course, when suddenly cruel Death bade me halt and stopped the journey I had started. I pleaded my strength and wealth, my flower of youth, my wife's tears and my father's sad prayers. But my words fell upon deaf ears, inflexible Death drew his weapon and laid me low with cruel wounds. But why speak I of myself? So many sons lie here buried in the earth, but their spirits ascend to the stars. While thou readest this, pity my fate and say a propitious prayer. My present fate may soon perhaps be yours".

Once again his effigy is on the top of the tomb complete save for the loss of half his sword.

On the top of the chest tomb under a protective carpet covering lie two fine brasses to William Fermor (1552) and his wife Elizabeth Norrys.

At the west end of the chapel, which was a chantry for the Fermor family are three fine white marble memorials, while at the east end is a tiny piscina almost hidden by the tomb.

It's not all memorials to the Fermors in the chapel however for there is a black memorial to Thomas Morgan who is referred to as having 'Great Morgan's name'.

Equally interesting is the early 14th century stone reredos behind the altar depicting the Last Supper with St John lying in the lap of Jesus. It is made of Brize Norton stone and is similar to one

at Bampton. It has a curious history, for like so many fine carvings and murals it was hidden from the Puritans in the 17th century and was only recovered from its burial place and restored in 1822!

Other memorials include a tablet to John Collingridge who died in 1698 aged 28, and a more recent one to William Barnes of Great Duryard, Exeter, who was Patron of Somerton. He was the son of Samuel Barnes, who was the sixth son of Archdeacon Ralph Barnes. Juliana Speke the daughter of William Speke of Jordans, Somerset is also recorded on the same memorial so there is a West Country link with the church.

There is another 17th century memorial to William Mynn who died in 1665 and his wife Mary who died four years later.

The 18th century memorial to Elizabeth Watson is specially interesting because the stonemason obviously miscalculated the width of the name, and had to carve a tiny letter 'n' at the end of it, a third the size of the rest of the surname to make it fit on the stone after he had carved WATSO!

The oldest stained glass is in the north wall – crimson and yellow with coats of arms, although there are 14th century windows in the chancel, the same age as the three sedilia.

The stained glass in the east window is Victorian and highly colourful, while the glass in the east end of the north aisle is of the same period but much more restrained.

There are three exceptionally fine Jacobean chairs in the church but happily there is strong security to protect them!

The church itself dates from 1075, being built shortly after the Norman conquest, but all that remains of the original building is the doorway now blocked up in the south wall of the nave. The single flanged key remains and hangs behind glass – it was regularly in use until 1993!

The chancel screen is finely carved, and the choir stalls have some fascinating and varied carvings of all kinds of animals, plus two exceptional carvings of children on the ends.

Look upwards in the nave to see the stone corbels and of course, the Tudor clerestory, with a splendid timber roof.

There is a 14th century font which is unusually narrow and on a hexagonal mount.

Externally, the tower with its eight pinnacles, reminiscent of Deddington church, was built in the late 1300s, and on the north side is a remarkable carved stone Holy Rood depicting Christ on the Cross under a tracery canopy, probably added early in the reign of Edward III.

Some sizeable gargoyles glower over the churchyard, and a rough stone arch of slotted stones above one of the nave windows which does not correspond to any of the better known architectural styles. The shape is flattened Norman, but could it have been earlier – Saxon perhaps? The other windows represent a glorious mixture of styles which make this church even more interesting.

A high cross in the churchyard remains and must have been the scene of outdoor worship on many occasions in the past. Once again because Somerton is at a crossing point one can imagine pilgrims gathering here.

Like all churches the upkeep takes a lot of money, and St James's is no exception. However there's good news for the people of Somerton for the clock is soon to become automatic. It has been run electrically for some time, but any fluctuation in the power supply in the past led to considerable inaccuracy until the late Mr Hill arrived to put it right. Mr Hill is now in heaven, so he is no longer available to rectify any bad timekeeping.

Now to mark the Millennium it will soon run perfectly again hopefully to record the next 1,000 years for this village and its most imposing and decorative church.

The Magic of St Michael's at Great Tew

STUNNING, magical and exciting – hardly the words that the sophisticated reader might expect to be used to describe one of our Oxfordshire churches, but that was my immediate reaction on first seeing St Michael's at Great Tew.

I suppose thousands of people visit the beautiful village, but I wonder just how many drive on up the hill and pause at the ornate archway at the roadside which is the entrance to the church. They could be excused for missing St Michael's however, for it is invisible from the road, but I urge anyone who enjoys reading these articles to make the effort of walking 400 or so yards down a grassy drive.

The first sign that you are getting near are the tombstones on the left behind a walled sunken garden, and then suddenly in a dip you see the beautiful church of St Michael and

• *The lady in contemplative mood is Mary Ann Boulton, the statue of which was executed by Sir Francis Chantry, a famous 19th century sculptor.*

All Angels, with its 15th century clerestory windows, and its reflective Cotswold stone.

I suppose it had more effect on me because I set out from Middleton Cheney looking for the non-existing Clifton church (it was de-consecrated some 30 years ago), and so I drove on to Hempton, where it was too difficult to park. Ever onward with Swerford

78

in mind, but then I saw the turn to Great Tew, and the search was on. Of course I expected St Michael's to be in the village, but after some help I discovered it, at the top of the hill to the south.

It's always a gamble whether a church will be open when one gets there, but both north and south doors at St Michael's were wide open welcoming the sunshine, the refreshing breeze, and visitors like me.

I went in by the exquisite south porch – exquisite because of its Norman carving, its scalloped archway, and its curved stone seats, along with cressets which are hollows scooped out for wicks to float on melting fat.

Another gamble for me is wondering what the door will reveal. Will it be a restored building with much of the original missing, or will it be full of history, and that indefinable sense of wonder that so much mystery has remained?

St Michael's is one of the latter. True I was lucky to see it on one of those days when the clouds scudded across the sky so that shafts of brilliant sunlight streamed through the clear paned windows, and one of them lit up the particularly fine 15th century font.

Behind the font was a board which recorded that the church was restored in 1827 at a cost of £1,489.12s and the chancel at £2,096.9s.9d.

Next to the nearest pillar to the font is a four foot tall carved black wooden eagle which supports a lectern with a selection of biblical references to help visitors with any day to day problems they might face.

By the lofty south arch is a tablet which records how Edm Hiorns of New Woodstock, who died in 1627 gave £5 for the 'poore of the town of Great Tew'.

'Town?' – well not so strange, for in 1100, the church known as Ciric Tiwa (Church Tew) was part of one of the largest manors in Oxfordshire, and was mentioned in a will of 1009.

Thomas Fletcher of Great Tew who died in 1641 also left £5 for the poor to be paid out on Good Friday, as did John Sly of Little Tew, who died in 1657.

(Did Shakespeare know of the Sly family when he wrote Much Ado one wonders?).

There are two fine arcades supported by early 14th century pillars which stand on earlier bases, and there is evidence of Norman stonework at the base of the tower, and a small infilled window on the north side of the church.

The first recorded incumbent was Walter, Chaplain of Hafidd, whose patron in 1244 was Ralph de Pratell.

The church in Norman times probably had two chantry chapels to judge from the piscinas at the east end of the south wall, and the one now in the vestry.

Also in the north side of the vestry almost hidden by chairs and candle tapers is the stone effigy of an early 14th century knight who deserves more exposure. However the vestry is kindly left open for the visitor to see the knight, who is more than a bit special, for he is one of only four similar effigies now remaining in England to have ailettes on their shoulders.

Eanswythe Hunter who wrote the extensive guide to the church (well worth £1!) believes the other three are at Maltby, Clehongre, and Ashby Sandwich. The knight is believed to be Robert de Vere, a Great Tew landowner.

Nearby also in the north wall is the effigy of a lady believed to be Margery Dyve, the Abbess of Godstow, 1316-1355, and probably the widow of Sir Robert. The village had links with Godstow Abbey from 1302 until the Dissolution.

The pride and joy of the chancel is the beautifully sculpted marble tomb to Mary Anne Boulton (1795-1829) wife of Matthew Robinson Boulton, who commissioned the famous sculptor Sir Francis Chantrey to carve her effigy in 1834. A work of art on its own account, it made the whole visit to Great Tew worthwhile.

Opposite the memorial on the south wall is

another piece of history – a tablet erected in 1885 to Lucius Carey, Viscount Falkland, Secretary of State to Charles I who 'fell fighting at the side of the King at the Battle of Newbury on September 20th, 1643'. He died when he was 34, but he lived at Tew and attracted a society of learned friends. The church register records his burial at Great Tew, and that of his wife, Lettice, his sons, Lorenzo, Lucius and Harry, the third and fourth Viscounts. There are no tombs, but they are believed to be buried under the chancel as the lead lined coffin of Harry was found during the 19th century repairs to this part of the church.

• *St Michael's is not visible from the road, but nestles in a hollow to the left of the carriageway that led to the Manor. There used to be formal gardens on either side of what is now a grass covered track, although remains of the walled beds still remain. The gardens and trees were planted and laid out in the time of Lucius Carey, Viscount Falkland, Secretary of State to the ill-fated Charles I.*

Still on the south wall of the chancel by the altar, and immediately in front of the tall sedilia, are wall mounted brasses to Sir John and Lady Alice Wilcotes (1410) and William and Agnes Busby (1513) and there is a trinity brass and inscription (1487) for William Reynsford.

Embroiderers will love the chancel carpet which was made in 1955 by the Woodstock Embroidery Guild, and the hassocks made by children at Great Tew school to the design of Mrs Bury, the headteacher of the school, in 1960.

The church is full of ornate wood carving, especially the 15th century pew ends which all have subtle differences. More superb carving in the three decker pulpit and part of the covered entrance to the upper from the vestry has part of the original screen incorporated.

When I was a little boy, together with my sister, we used to play trains in Lancing church in Sussex pretending that the box pews were carriages with doors, so it was a treat to see similar box pews at St Michael's. They were made in the 19th century for the Great Tew estate servants.

There's a link with Ireland in the chancel through the memorial to Mrs Frances Hayes who was the daughter of Sir James Hayes, a member of the Irish Privy Council in the 17th century.

Back to the church and look heavenwards and note all the fine faces in the corbels, and the particularly fine nave ceiling which is the work of Thomas Rickman in 1827, using a method of painting plaster to make it look like wood.

I know readers like to hear about the bells and the organ, and at St Michael's there are eight bells which we are told are of 'particularly fine tone'. Bells one, two, four, six and seven were given by Sir Anthony Keck in 1709 and cast by Abraham Rudhall. Number Three was cast in 1785, and number five in 1842. The tenor, bell eight, was cast in 1709 and weighs 22 cwt. The organ is two manual and dates from the early 19th century.

Because it was probably the most traumatic period in Britain's history for the effect it had on rural families, war memorials are always affecting, and the one at St Michael's is among the best. They too are fascinating historical records, for the men from Great Tew who fell included those from local regiments – the Oxfordshire and Buckinghamshire LI, the Oxfordshire Yeomanry – but also from the Canadian Mounted Rifles, and one Corporal F.Hartley, who died in the ill fated expedition to aid the White Russian forces in Russia against the revolutionaries in 1919.

There's lots more to see, but as I emerged into the sunshine, I was greeted by the biggest ginger cat I have yet seen, sunning itself on an ancient 17th century tomb, and as I walked to the ornate gateway to leave I saw the plaque saying it was restored in 1992 to the memory of Eustace Robb, and I recalled another magical visit to Great Tew.

I was then writing for the Oxford Mail and doing a piece about the estate, and Major Robb invited me to share a plate of strawberries and cream (tough being a reporter then!). It was everything a plate of English strawberries should be but with an added flavour which made it exceptional. The secret?

Major Robb told me it had a dash of cointreau, and no strawberries of mine have been without it since, so he has my undying gratitude.

Yes, lots of magic at Great Tew, and as I left the full crescent moon was appearing opposite the sun – and I could almost swear the cat winked at me!

Great Tew's world famous wall paintings

OXFORDSHIRE churches are well known for their wall paintings, but no-one knows why there should be so many. However there must have been teams of painters with varying skills working throughout the county around the same time, each one organised by a master painter.

The ones at Great Tew are worth a visit on their own account. Those in the south aisle of the Passion (part of which are pictured upper right) were uncovered in 1988, and were dated in the 1300s.

The style of the paintings in Great Tew is unique in Oxfordshire, being much cruder than those at South Newington which *Four Shires* chronicled in an earlier edition. But, as another booklet specifically about the paintings (again well worth £1) records: "the drawing executed in red, pink and black lines is remarkable, since the artist took little account of scale or proportion, being more intent on composition. It suggests a rather unskilled draughtsman copying compositions from another source with little understanding of the anatomy being suggested by the original artist".

At the time when the paintings were begun, Great Tew villagers would have been severely affected by Edward I's wars against France, Scotland and Wales, the 1315 famine and the Black Death.

Few in the congregation could read or write or understand the Latin of the clergy, and they learned about Christianity from the pictures on the walls –which must have been rather like today's TV programmes are to us.

St Michael's, with its sizeable nave, would also have provided a good stage for the Miracle Plays, and the wall paintings an effective stage background. Interestingly Oxford at the time was one of the most important centres for the illumination of sacred books, and William of Brailes had a workshop there.

The scene at the top of the wall which looks like St Michael weighing souls before their owners were consigned to heaven or hell must have had quite an impression on the worshippers!

Our picture (right) shows the wall paintings in black and white as Rachel Maxwell-Hyslop visualises them in the

• *This is the lower right section of the wall painting as it appears today in the church in red, pink and black.*

booklet. The pictures show the weighing of souls, the entry into Jerusalem, the washing of feet, the betrayal, the crowning with thorns, Pontius Pilate, the flagellation, carrying the cross, the crucifixion, the deposition, the entombment, the harrowing of hell, the resurrection, and 'Noli me Tangere'.

What is so good is that there are probably many, many more wall paintings to be uncovered and restored in the church – providing thousands of visitors to St Michael's can spare the odd coin or two towards discovery and restoration.

Meet Wills Campiun, Master Mason, the man who built Helmdon Church

IT was a sad occasion that first led me to the church of St Mary Magdalene at Helmdon, but ultimately a happy one.

Sad because I went to the funeral of Sue Gidman. Sue had worked with me at the very start of the Banbury Cake newspaper, and as she was a much-loved member of the Helmdon community, the church was packed for the service.

Happy because once we had all said our farewells there was a chance for me to look at the church and see its beauty; and so I returned a few weeks later to learn more about this 12th century church which was built from stone quarried in the village itself.

We know that one of the masons was Wills (William) Campiun for he is commemorated in a small segment at the top of the window in the north aisle which is closest to the chancel.

There he is with stone mason's sharp edged mallet in hand and an inscription which reads

• *Detail from the fine east window which was installed in 1917 and which bears comparison with the best stained glass anywhere.*

Will's: Campiun: Fecit: Hoc: Op: Lapi: Dis Anno Dni MCCCXIII, which shows that our Wills worked on the fabric of the church in 1313.

The actual window is of exceptional interest as it is one of the very few English mediaeval windows to depict an artisan with the tools of his trade. The only others are in York Minster and St George's Chapel at Windsor.

The leading of the window which was almost intact before the window was conserved in 1976-7 is preserved behind glass in a frame on the north wall. It was too weak to be re-used so the window is now safely preserved in new lead.

Helmdon has other similar fine small mediaeval stained glass at the tops of the windows in the north and south aisles, and Wills is in good company for the arms of the Earls and first Duke of Lancaster, and the Warennes Earls of Surrey are

• *St Mary Magdalene church at Helmdon with the nature conservation area in the foreground.*

displayed, along with scraps of former windows which are above the Lady altar in the south aisle.

However the finest window is in the east behind the altar. Commemorating the death of Florence Wonnacott, the wife of a Rector, in December 1913, it was installed in 1917 and represents from left to right, the birth of Christ, his death and resurrection, and while one usually just absorbs the overall effect of a stained glass window, this one bears closer study. The work, especially in the faces is exquisite, and at least proves that glass makers in the early 20th century more than equalled that of the great Victorians.

The church, like so many in the *Four Shires* was thoughtfully restored by those Victorians in 1874 and retained many of the original features.

For instance the fine three seated stepped sedilia in the chancel has some splendid decorated hood mouldings, and there are mediaeval carvings of heads abounding, and while they could be members of the same family, one stopped me short in my tracks. For quite clearly there was one of a long eared dog – and immediately I felt a glow of admiration for the family who had obviously loved their pooch so much that they had immortalised their pet in stone.

The church has three piscinae (the stone bowls where the communion vessels were washed). There is a finely decorated one by the sedilia, a much smaller one (originally on the other side of the chancel) which is just inside the door of the north porch, and another in the exterior north wall by the vestry building corner, which provides a home for a nesting bird. That one could have been in the wall of a former chapel, or it could have been used for services outside the church during the times of the lepers and plagues.

84

• *These small windows are all that are left of the original mediaeval glass, and some depict the arms of famous families, such as the Earls and first Duke of Lancaster, and the Warennes Earls of Surrey.*

The south porch has very sensibly been turned into toilets, and there are kitchen facilities. When our churches are nowadays returning to part of their original function in mediaeval times as social meeting places, they are essential, but one wonders what the privy arrangements were centuries ago.

The two porches were built in the 15th century, while the original church was the nave which was built in the 12th century. The chancel is 13th century, and the tower was rebuilt in 1823 after it had been struck by lightning, although the useful notes about the church in a freely available pamphlet declares that it was a copy of the original which was built in the 14th century.

• *It takes 1,700 years to produce the patterns on the giant trunk of the yew that dominates the churchyard.*

In the belfry are six bells and the oldest were cast in 1679 – the tenor has an inscription which reads: "That all may cvm and non may stay at hom, I ring to sermon with a lusty bom. 1679".

Moving back to the chancel there is a single manual organ built by Henry Jones, of Fulham Road, London, with a thoughtful memorial plaque to Marjorie Rose Brown, organist, who died on March 16th 1977.

Little, one suspects, remains of the original chancel floor, for the 18th century memorial tombstones are almost worn away, and while the church itself was built with local Helmdon stone, much of the floor appears to have been laid much later with Hornton blue stone.

The four clerestory windows on the north of the nave and the three on the south side have their original glass, and for those interested in church architecture the pillars form an interesting comparison. Those on the north side - 18 inches in diameter with octagon capitals are rather finer, and appear later than the south side with their 21 inch quatrefoil capitals.

It was not too easy to get to the mural tomb in the south wall because some genial workmen (could they have been Wills' descendants one wonders?) were working on the porch housing the kitchen, but we are told it is covered with black granite with traces of ornamentation.

85

However by the time this appears in print I am sure you will be able to see for yourselves if you take the trip to this charming Northamptonshire village near Brackley.

However, clearly visible above the Early English arch keystone is the stone helmeted head in the style of those worn for the crusades, so it's a reasonable assumption that the tomb is of some long forgotten Helmdon crusader.

During the Victorian restoration the musicians' gallery in the west end under the tower was removed – probably when the organ was installed, and another Victorian item is the rugged font by the north door.

Have a look at the fine kneelers which were created by a large number of people in the last decade of the last century.

The church guide says: "The overall colours have been chosen to tone with the nave windows, and the chancel carpet, but the designs have been the choice of both workers and sponsors, to remember many individuals and village organisations and buildings. The smaller and differently coloured Noah's Ark kneelers were stitched by pupils in Helmdon School".

However to see the many designs you do not have to turn them all over they have been preserved in albums by the church door which have colour photographs of them all.

Walk round the outside of the church and prepare to be amazed by the massive yew tree at the east end of the church. The Conservation Foundation Country Living Yew Tree Campaign certifies that it is at least 1,700 years old! The trunk is between eight to nine feet in diameter, and it has marvellous natural growth designs. You will have to walk under the exterior branches which almost touch the ground to see the trunk, but it's well worth the trouble.

One tree you just can't ignore is the stark remains of a fir tree at the edge of the churchyard which points its ragged fingers to the skies.

There are many monuments, many of them to farmers and schoolmasters on the exterior of the walls, plaques recording the tower restoration, and on the stone of the south porch, with many more carved heads above the windows.

The churchyard is one of the largest I have yet come across in a village and is beautifully maintained. It was good to see beautiful lawns alongside the area on the south side which has tall grasses allowed to grow freely in a conservation area, and which encourages a variety of lichens. The air must be good!

There are seats at good vantage points, and lovely views for contemplation. Alongside many ornamental stones from the 17th century and later, I came across a very simple wooden cross which had the name George Batchelor picked out in scrabble tiles, and one hopes George is now happily adding up his scores in heaven.

Finally, because the church, with its memorials to its farmers, is so much a rural sanctuary, I was taken by this sampler inside the church, called The Farmer's Prayer. It reads:

"Let the wealthy and great
Roll in splendour and state
I envy them not I declare it.
I eat my own lamb, my chicken and ham,
I shear my own fleece and wear it.
I have lawns, I have bow'rs
I have fruits, I have flow'rs.
The lark is my morning alarmer
So jolly boys now
Here's God speed the plough
Long life and success to the farmer".

You might think this was some relic from the 17th-18th century (and the poem may well be) but it was worked by Ann and Tony Smith in Helmdon in 2000 – and good health to them both for sharing it with us.

Don't look for exciting murals at Tysoe church — the only one that remains is a faint linear design, and to be frank I never actually found it. But the parish church, which is very rare in having kept its ancient dedication to the Assumption of the Blessed Virgin Mary, is a grade I building and it has some fine brasses. There is a great deal to see, so visit when you have some time to spare.

Now Tysoe, or Tiu's eye, which I believe was the derivation of its name, is very ancient. Legend has it that Tiu was a Saxon god well

The church at Tui's eye

before Christianity, and that there was a great red horse carved in the Edge Hill scarp above the village. Sadly nothing remains of the horse, but the excellent church guide suggests that the church may well stand on the site of a Romano-Celtic temple.

There was little to recall either pagans or Romans as I arrived, for one of several jet planes roared overhead shattering the calm, and almost at once it began to rain to freshen the sultry air outside.

• The new stained glass window installed in 1998 commemorates the work of Tysoe firemen.

Inside the church however there was no need for moist breezes for it was gloriously cool, and that ambience was emphasised by the beautiful blue of the cassocks, lovingly embroidered, and placed on the tops of the pews - clearly this church has a caring congregation.

But back to early days — Tysoe originally belonged to a great Saxon lord called Waga, who was dispossessed of his lands which were given to Robert de Stafford. In the

Domesday Book it was a place of some importance for it had 23 hides (2300 acres) of land and it was rated at £32 — a sizeable sum in those days — and in 1279 Nicholas de Stafford had 13 tenants and his son, Robert, saw this grow to 19.

Ralph Lord Stafford, who was Steward to the household of Edward III in 1342, was granted a weekly market on Tuesdays, and an annual four day fair on August 1st, the Feast Day of

• Detail from the font. St Catherine with her wheel.

St Peter in Chains. Tysoe was also important enough to have the Knights Templar on its land, and it must have been a good place for hunting, for in 1285 Nicholas de Stafford had Free Warren, or the right to take deer or game on the lands near the village.

There's a brilliant church guide, which is crammed with information, and you'll need some time to see everything of interest in this impressive building which dates back to the eleventh century - there was a priest mentioned in the Domesday Book.

Go in through the fifteenth century south porch but keep the outer door open so you can see the twelfth century carved Norman doorway, with a carved Paschal lamb between a mask and a beak, which is believed to have come from an earlier doorway.

Children will like the stone carved dog's head with its tongue out, at the wall almost facing the doorway, and nearby there is a headless Norman horseman, best seen from the west side. It's easy to see the original walls of the early church for there are windows out into the south aisle inside what is now the main church building.

Anyone wanting to stage a Shakespearean play with the actors in the clothes of the time need look no further than the reclining effigy of a former patron of the church. William Clark, who was a former patron, is resplendently attired in full Tudor dress. If the wardrobe

• The stunning 15th century font with its carved wooden canopy.

department needs to see what a lady of the time wore, then they need look no further than the brass half-effigy to Jane Gibbs who died in 1598, which is behind the pulpit. Near to Jane is the brass engraving of the shield of arms of Tomizane, who died in 1611. They were both married to Nicholas Browne.

Another brass just past the north door commemorates a priest, Thomas Mastrupe, who died in the mid fifteenth century.

The association of the Knights Templar - they lived in Temple Tysoe - is marked by the oldest stained glass in the church, which can only be seen through the empty pierced stone screen in the chancel.

It depicts a monk's head, and it was probably that of St Nicholas of Tolentino, an Augustine who was associated with the Knights Templar and the Canons of Stone who held the church at one time.

There was once a rood screen, and if there are children with you they will be intrigued by the tiny wooden door behind the pulpit, which once led to the screen which has long since gone.

There's a 14th century tomb with a coffin lid marked by a long cross in the north wall, behind a prie dieu in front of a recess beneath the war memorial, and a large 17th century churchwarden's chest at the west end of the north aisle.

One of the best features of the church is the remarkable 14th century font with its carvings of God on his throne, St Peter, St Catherine with her wheel, St John the Baptist baptising Jesus, the Madonna and Child, the Archangel Michael, Mary Magdalen with her pot of precious ointment, and St Paul the Apostle with a sword.

Herring-bone masonry above the two splayed windows suggests a Saxon origin, and for people who are fond of pews there are four original Elizabethan seats around the font. There's also a fine coat of arms for those who collect them.

Excellent old stained glass attracts the eye, but one with real village history is the fine new window dedicated to the Tysoe Fire Station. It was installed as recently as 1998, after the County Council closed the Fire Station which had given Tysoe and the surrounding villages a century of service. It was put together using rare traditional English methods which reflect the vivid reds and blues which cannot be achieved by modern glass. The twelfth century tower has three stages and is now home to several varieties of birds who weave and soar around the battlements. It houses six bells which date from 1719 to 1782.

Note the eighteenth century bell-cote at the other end to the tower, and try and work out the time from the ancient sundial on the porch. There are masses of interesting tombstones, and some truly gruesome gargoyles and masks - these also will please children who love to be scared!

The church however is truly welcoming for if you wish you can see the silver by appointment, and if you are a bellringer, you may also ring the bells. What's more, if you want to visit the church as a party then Mrs Chris Locke (01295 680251) or Mrs Mim Kitchen (01295) 680274 can supply refreshments by appointment. I would go just for Chris' cakes! Tysoe repays close study and I came away feeling there was so much more to see if only I had had the time. It certainly has an air of satisfaction about it. "I've been here for at least one millennium" it seems to say "and people worshipped here for a millennium before that, so jet planes disturbing my peace have no more significance that a gnat whining on an autumn evening".

Go and see it for yourself - it's well worth it.

90

Oxfordshire's first cathedral is now Dorchester

DON'T be fooled by the deceptive entrance to Dorchester Abbey, for although the timber lychgate is magnificent in its own right, it is dated 1867 and effectively obscures the transitional Norman church.

And while it's the parish church for Dorchester on Thames, it is also a fine abbey building, and is on or near the site of a Saxon cathedral which was erected in the seventh century.

Oxfordshire is therefore lucky in that it has two cathedrals – Christ Church in Oxford City – and the less ornate, but equally impressive, abbey church of St Peter and St Paul on the banks of the Thames. The county's churches also have two Bishops, the Bishop of Oxford and the Bishop of Dorchester, and the latter has the weight of an impressive history behind him.

It was in 635 that Oswald of Northumbria, overlord of the Anglo-Saxon kingdoms who was a great Christian king, met the pagan king of Cynegils of Wessex, near Dorchester.

The kings celebrated two great events, the proposed marriage of Cynegils' daughter to Oswald, and Cynegils' baptism, with Oswald as sponsor, by a missionary bishop named Birinus. Birinus had been sent to England by Pope Honorious I with the aim of sowing the seeds of faith in the most remote regions of the English. But when he arrived in 635 in Wessex he found

• *Pictured alongside (left) is the world famous Tree of Jesse window, combining tracery, sculpture and glass in a single window. It shows the descent of Christ from Jesse.*

• *The 19th century lychgate is the main entrance to the Abbey, which appears hidden behind it. Pass through it, however, and you will find a museum on the left and the Abbey in front of you.*

the West Saxons so heathen he decided to stay among them.

As a result of the marriage, the two kings gave Bishop Birinus the city of Doric (Dorchester) for his episcopal see, and he built several churches, one of which was his cathedral.

Birinus became a saint, and was buried in Dorchester, but when war with the northern kingdom of Mercia seemed certain, his relics were taken to Winchester.

West Mercia in turn was invaded by the Danes and in 869 Dorchester became the seat of a vast Mercian see which stretched from the Thames to the Humber.

Wulfwig was the last Saxon bishop and he died in 1067. He was succeeded by the only Norman bishop of Dorchester, Remigius, who moved his seat to Lincoln, and it was Alexander of Lincoln who refounded the church as an abbey for Augustinian canons, and the nave of the present building is the west end of that Norman building.

The tomb of St Birinus was opened in 1225 and the abbey became a place of pilgrimage and was enlarged in 1293, and a shrine to the saint was added around 1340. The present tower was erected in 1602.

Before that however, the abbey was dissolved by Henry VIII, and the shrine was destroyed. Luckily the monastic part of the church was bought by Richard Beauforest, who was 'a great riche man' of Dorchester, for use

91

• *The magnificent nave and chancel is dominated by the great east window, which is divided by a central pillar and filled throughout with flowing tracery in unusual patterns. It shows scenes from the life of Christ.*

by the people of the parish who thus inherited a glorious church.

To see it, pass through the lychgate, or walk round the corner through the churchyard, enter the wood balustraded porch, and open the small door. Then be astounded by the proportions of the People's Chapel which was alongside the monastic abbey. The altar is raised on a four stair platform above a burial vault with a 14th century wall painting of a crucifixion with the figures of St Mary and St John and the sun and the moon. Above that are the remains of a doom wall painting, and a blocked up window. There's also a small doorway which looks as if it was an entrance to the Lady Chapel and St Birinus' tomb.

Wonderfully vaulted arches lead to the nave and chancel, but before moving on have a look at the fine 12th century lead font which is one of the finest in England.

Inset in the floors are interesting inscribed tombstones. One is to Sarah Fletcher unable to 'bear the rude Shakes and jostlings which we met with in this transitory World, Nature gave way; she sunk and died a Martyr to Excessive sensibility in 1799 in her 29th year".

Another is to Michael Desvaupons, d.1798, Archdeacon of Dol in Brittany, a Roman Catholic refugee from the French Revolution. (Dorchester apparently treated English Roman Catholics with considerable tolerance even after the Dissolution and there is a strong link today between the religious communities).

Of special interest to the north of the county is the stone commemorating Francis Dandridge, d.1714, a relative of Martha Dandridge, the second wife of George Washington of Sulgrave.

Americans have been very generous to the abbey, for the great east window was restored by American friends of the abbey in 1966 in memory of Sir Winston Churchill, and the lychgate, in memory of Edith Stedman, was restored in 1981.

Once in the nave and chancel, the breathtaking great east window dominates the view, with the magnificent arcades which are perfectly composed.

Look too, at the big three manual organ by Walkers of London, which is in the north wall and completely dissociated from the choir stalls. This may well change when the abbey undergoes a £5m regeneration in the future.

Part of this regeneration will see the shrine of St Birinus as the focus of a transformed Lady Chapel, which contains some nationally important mediaeval effigies.

The earliest and most famous is the late 13th century knight in freestone. The knight wears mail and a surcoat, and is recumbent on his back but twisted in the act of drawing his sword. He has a lion at his feet, and he is particularly important because of the pose, which is lively. The great sculptor, Henry Moore, was said to have been influenced by the movement in this work.

More traditionally in repose is the 14th century knightly figure in alabaster. It has a finely carved helmet, with an ornamental bank of linked roses and pendant mail defence for the neck known as an aventail. Once again he has a lion at his feet.

There are two more effigies – the 14th century mitred figure of a bishop discovered beneath the floor in the 18th century – and Chief Justice of Common Pleas, Sir John de Stonore, who died in 1354. He was buried in the chancel where his memorial stood until it was restored in the 19th century.

The actual shrine has long since disappeared but the memorial to Bishop Gerald Allen, the first Suffragan Bishop of Dorchester, dedicated in 1964, suggests the form of the original, and the canopy contains fragments of the original vaulting found in a walled up doorway in 1870.

Also in the Lady Chapel is the Union Flag used for the funerals of British soldiers who were prisoners of war at Kuching in Borneo, and is there in memory of members of the 35th Light Anti-Aircraft regiment of the Royal Artillery. Read the interesting story about it.

Readers always like to know about the bells, and the seventh (13cwt) was cast in 1375 by the Exeter foundry, and the tenor (16cwt) of a similar date was cast by the mediaeval Wokingham foundry.

It has the inscription: "Do

What do you think of this painting by Roger Wagner? Entitled 'Menorah' it has been placed in Dorchester Abbey after the Bishop of Oxford suggested it might be a suitable setting for permanent housing.

The Bishop said: "Roger Wagner is one of the most outstanding artists of our time painting on Christian themes. His Menorah will, I believe, prove to be one of the outstanding paintings of the late 20th century".

Visitors to the Abbey have been invited to make their comments on the painting, the idea for which came when the artist was travelling by train from Oxford to London.

The sense of human vulnerability in the face of great mechanistic forces led to the idea of placing the crucifixion scene in the foreground. It was only later that the artist saw in the six towers and one chimney the symmetrical appearance of the seven-branched candelabrum, the menorah, which is a central Jewish symbol of God's presence.

Why place it in Dorchester Abbey? The late John Harriott said: "Didcot Power station carries light and power to roughly the area where Birinus carried the light and power of the Christian faith. It smacks, like all power stations, of up-to-date 20th century modernity. It seems more important to our daily life than a Roman missionary of centuries ago. But, in 1400 years from now will it even be a scar on the grass? Will it be remembered with honour and affection? Will it be a place of pilgrimage?"

thou Birinus protect forever those when I summon. Ralph Restwold." The 5cwt third bell was cast by the Knights at the Reading foundry in 1651, the fourth (6cwt) was cast in 1603, and the 5th (7cwt) in 1591. They all have a Protection Order and may not be recast or rehung separately.

When you leave the abbey – and you should allow an hour to see the interior with its stone coffins, superb windows, paintings, and stone carvings – you will pass the Guest House.

This was originally joined to the tower which has two corner turrets of chequer patterned flint and stone, and an interior 14th century spiral staircase.

The Guest House is now a museum for both the abbey and the area, is open from May to September except Mondays, and at Easter, and you can enjoy refreshments served by abbey volunteers.

Hopefully any money raised goes to the Dorchester Abbey Campaign, supported by worthies ranging from the Archbishop of Canterbury to Anne Heseltine of Thenford.

Lord Runcie says: "Dorchester is a nodal point in the development of faith in the people of these islands. We need to guard its treasures".

93

IT's probably the oldest church in Oxfordshire, built almost at the same time as the glorious Dorchester Abbey, and with the exception of Overthorpe, near Banbury, it's the most difficult to find! Not because it is inaccessible, but because Enstone Church is not really at Enstone at all, but at least a mile away at Church Enstone – however, despite that it's well worth a visit.

And it's another of those churches that has had an identity crisis in the past .

Dedicated originally as St Kenelm's in AD 820, it was re-dedicated to St Edward the Confessor in 1382, and it retained that Kingly name, until 1930 when it reverted to being St Kenelm's – and although that took

The home of St Kenelm - 'the Cotswold Saint'

place in quite modern times in terms of history there's no record of any re-dedication.

So who was St Kenelm? Again we have two versions. One says he was the son of King Kenulphas who founded the Abbey Church on the site of a nunnery at Winchcombe in 811. The other has it that St Cynhelm was the son of Cenwulf who died around 1812 and was buried at Winchcombe. As King Kenulphas was also buried at Winchcombe, it's probably just a confusion of names. What is not in doubt is the legend of the death of King Kenelmus (St Cynhelm) at the hand of his sister in 819.

In the legend, a dove took the news of

• *A tree in full leaf almost obscures the west window in the tower*

Kenelm's death to the Pope, who had his remains dug up and re-buried at Winchcome Abbey.

He was canonised, his relics venerated and his cult was popular throughout the Middle Ages, with July 17th being celebrated as St Kenelm's Day.

In the year after his death, Enstone's first

• *The south aspect of St Kenelm's church.*

small Saxon church was dedicated to him by the Abbot of Winchcombe Abbey, and a shrine was established to him in the Abbey itself. Later the Abbey was dedicated to the Virgin Mary and St Kenelm by the Bishop of Worcester.

Known as the Cotswold Saint, St Kenelm has seven Cotswold churches dedicated to him – and why he fell out of favour at Enstone for St Edward we shall never know.

All traces of the Saxon church have now gone but before 1223, Walter de Bannebir (Banbury) was the first Rector. He was replaced in that year by a Kentish man, William de Kentis, to be followed by the exotically named Geoffrey de Sancto Medardo in 1272. A good Oxfordshire Rector, William de Wykeham followed him, and became the last of the Rectors, as the incumbents have all been Vicars ever since.

However, there was a church on the site in 1175, and the present south aisle with its five wide arches, all with different carved capitals at the top of the pillars, was added to the original church and superseded it as the main building.

The south doorway with its superb Norman zigzag design is a fine example of its type.

Along came the north aisle in 1280, with two scalloped pillars and two round ones, and in 1320 the tower was built at the west end, and as if to balance the overall shape of the building, the chancel was added.

The church was still tied to Winchcombe Abbey and had a great Tithe Barn, built by Walter de Winfortune, alongside, so that the Abbot could collect all his tithes from the Enstone area. Over the years a Lady Chapel was added, plus a roof over the porch, and the south side extended, possibly for a tomb for the Abbot of Winchcombe.

We do not know about that however, because the tomb was destroyed in the Civil War, and that may have been the fate of the six small statues of saints in the reredos above the stone altar in the south chapel. They were also removed, along with another four full size saints and only their niches remain.

Happily however they did not bother to destroy the monument to Steven Wisdom, who died in 1633. Clad in his blue jacket he is kneeling looking in a somewhat macabre way at his own tombstone! Equally macabre for

those with modern sensitivities, is the stone coffin in the north aisle – made for someone of remarkable stature for the time as it is over six feet long. It has a hole in the centre of the base to allow the fluids from a decaying body to drain away.

Not quite as old, but certainly very ancient, is the wooden chest also in the north aisle.

As you enter the church by the magnificent south door, you can see a good painting of the church porch exterior by John Osborne, and on the north wall is a very fine war memorial window which has a large spray of poppies in front.

One of the fallen in the Great War was Wilfred Huckin, and one of the churchwardens in the 1980s was W.T.Huckin; and this reminded me at once of a lovely fellow pupil at Banbury County, then Grammar School, called Janet Huckin. It was an unusual name, and one I have not come across since. I wonder if Janet's family originally came from Church Enstone?

Anyway enough of schoolboy musings, and on to the bells, six of them dating from 1661 to 1769, and to the organ. There's a valuable framed history of

• *Steven Wisdom contemplates his own tombstone.*

96

the church in the north aisle, and when it was typewritten (sometime obviously before 1986) it recorded that the organ then had been built in 1886 and "required renewing".

The renewal turned into replacement and that obviously occurred, for the present electric Wyvern organ was first played on September 13th, 1987, by organist C.G.Edginton, in the presence of the Vicar, the Rev N.D.J.Carne, R.E.Williams (FRCO) the organ advisor, and churchwardens, J.M.Taylor, and W.T.Huckin – that memorable family name again.

The famous Victorian architect, G.E.Street, was responsible for a renovation of the chancel, and one suspects installed the stone pulpit which is very similar to others in nearby churches whose interiors he re-designed. The 14th century octagonal font however with its quatrefoil decoration remains the same as the time when some mediaeval stonemason first set chisel to it – probably after carving the trees of life on the summits of the south side pillars.

Another surname that recalled old memories was that of Benjamin Marten (the same name as that of Neil Marten, Banbury's excellent MP, who led the anti-Common Market campaign in the 1970s). Benjamin was an equally good man, for when he died in 1718, aged 47, he left a will which gave the income from property so that meat could be distributed to 20 poor people of Enstone, provided that five of them came from his home at nearby Radford.

He has a memorial on the north wall, and inset in front of the altar are memorials to four members of the Cole family, the first in 1678 to George Cole. There are a further six to the Walker family, and a strange one to Sir George Stonehouse, the only son of Sir John Stonehouse of Amerden Hall, in Essex, who was married to Dame Elizabeth Cole, the daughter of George Cole Esq of Buckish in Devon. It reads – "He departed this life on the 13th of April, 1695, aged 16" – which even allowing for the standards of the times, seems a bit young to have been married.

There's a superb brass lectern dedicated to Arthur, 16th Viscount Dillon, by his widow and

sons in 1892, and a spectacular window in the north wall to Harold Arthur, the 17th Viscount.

Another window in the east wall of the south chapel is dedicated to Ellen, Viscountess Dillon from Harold and Conrad.

Enstone's name is derived from the Saxon for giant (ent) and stan, a stone. The stone referred to is probably the 'Hoar Stone' which can still be seen at the junction of the Charlbury and Fulwell roads.

Enstone as a village was for many years a dependent enclave of the famous Benedictine Abbey at Winchcombe. It was King Kenulphas (Cenwulf) who reigned from 796 to 821, who gave the Abbey to the monastery. Enstone is mentioned in the Domesday Book as "Land of the Church of Winchcombe" and the Abbey at the time held 24 hides in the village.

The village was particularly famous in both the 17th and 18th centuries for its remarkable waterworks – a spring found by Thomas Bushell on his land in 1626 when he moved to the village. He and his family had an eye to the main chance for the waterworks and as such became famous and attracted many people.

A century after the discovery, the sound from the waterworks was described as imitating a nightingale's notes "contrived by the action of water pressing upon and expelling air from artificial tubes".

John Evelyn, the diarist, who was staying at Cornbury Park in 1664, wrote that he went by "chance to see the famous natural and artificial Grotto and Fountains called Bushell's Wells at Enstone. This Bushell had been secretary to Lord Verulam. It's an extraordinary solitude. There he had two mummies, a grotto, where he lay on a hammock like an Indian".

Despite being added to by the Earl of Lichfield of Ditchley Park, in 1674, the wells fell into disrepair and were destroyed in 1846.

So that was the end of Enstone Spa, but thankfully not of St Kenelm's or St Edward's – for whatever you care to call this church, it's yet another shining jewel in the Cotswold crown.

The village and church known by 100 names

ROLLENDRI, Rollendriche, Rollendru, Rolyndright, Rollyngrith, Boulandrigh, Rowlandright, Rowlandryght, Rolderche – all names for just one Oxfordshire village. And if you think that's a lot, then just consider that over 900 years that same village had a further 97 (!) variations on its name until 1791, when by general agreement the name became Rollright, and Rollright it has remained until the present day, with the prefixes Great and Little added to distinguish the two settlements. The full 106 names can be seen in the records in Brasenose College, which is the patron of the living of St Andrew's church, at Great Rollright. It was St Andrew's that we chose for this issue and after a series of dull, but warm overcast days it was a delight to see the sunshine, and even more of a delight to enjoy the fragrance of the pink roses lining the path to the impressive south porch which once had its own priest's room in the loft.

Impressive not only for its size, but for the stunning tympanum (the space between the lintel and the arch). It is a collection of amazing beak head mouldings and grotesque carvings,

one of which looks like a whale about to devour Jonah, although since the 'whale' appears to have breasts, and there are two bodies entwined, it might conceivably be Adam and Eve and the apple – but it's all in the eye of the beholder. Whatever, it's well worth a visit to the church for that alone.

The door opposite on the north wall of the original church is also well worth study with its zig zag moulding. This church is one of those where the original barn like structure can still be clearly seen, for it only has three wide arches on the south side, built when the Lady Chapel was erected. It has its own piscina (for washing the communion plate and vessels) but this is a very simple affair compared to the piscina in the chancel which is still painted in its original mediaeval colours, and reminds us of just how colourful church interiors used to be.

Another reminder of the use of bright colours can be seen in part of the roof just in front of the chancel which has survived deterioration over the years, and the restoration of that great

• A 20th century carved screen at the entrance to the tower is opposite the ancient rood screen to the chancel. This one was partially made by the Rev William Williams in memory of his mother, Elizabeth and his sister Mary.

Victorian ecclesiastical architect G.E.Street, whose influence can be seen in the chancel, which apart from the piscina is very plain. The names of some of the 45 Rectors can be seen in the Victorian floor tiles, but judging from the superb Decorated windows and the clerestory it must have been a much more ornate part of the church than it is now.

Luckily however the glorious gaily painted rood screen remains with its intricate carving, although the doorway leading to the rood loft above (long since gone) was blocked up.

There's a very fine wooden screen some 500 years newer leading to the tower and this was partially carved by the Rev William Guest Williams. He died in 1907 and the screen was in memory of his mother Elizabeth, and his sister, Mary.

Back in the chancel there are supports in each corner, for saints who would have stood there before the Reformation, or the Civil War, and a good brass with an interesting history. It shows a cleric with a Bishop's mitre on his vestment which indicated that the wearer, the Rev. Master James Batersby, who was a Rector of the church in 1522 had been offered a Bishopric but had refused it. Why, one wonders? There's a Latin inscription which tells us he was a Bachelor of Law and says 'May God have mercy on his soul. Amen'

Over the years there are many bequests to our churches but as a labour of love it would be hard to beat the framed illuminated poster history of St Andrew's, devised and illustrated by Joan Lawrence in 1994. It stands by the north door and visitors need to do no more than study it to see the life of St Andrew's over the years. If however you want to go into the history of the church in more depth, read the chapter in 'Rollright Past and Present' in the church. This sizable volume records the detailed story of the village published by the Great Rollright History Group at £13. However if you do not mind the binding being less than perfect you can snap up a copy from the village shop for just £7!

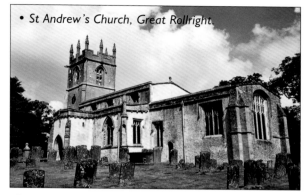

• *St Andrew's Church, Great Rollright.*

It contains masses of information, but perhaps the most fascinating, or gruesome, depending on your viewpoint is the Group's estimate that over 900 years some 4,100 bodies have been buried in the churchyard!

One of the most remarkable of these must have been a Rollright shepherd who died aged 104 in 1910, whose headstone lies just across the path from the very large early 20th century lych gate. This was erected by the nine sons of Mrs Rendall, the wife of the Rev Henry Rendall, Rector from 1885 to 1893, in her memory. The Rector is remembered by the clock on the tower.

Before the clock, villagers without their own timepieces, had to rely on the sundial which dates from 1658, on the south porch. Their eyes must however have strayed to the 47 carvings of heads, flowers and animals which run round the top of the porch and the south wall. The generally received opinion is that the human heads depicted those people who contributed to the church restoration in the 14th century – so nothing new there, for all our churches still remain constantly in need of restoration.

The vast majority of the stained glass is Victorian, and G.E.Street, or whoever, had a bit of fun with parishioners, for the East window has the saltire cross of St Andrew in small sections, which in themselves make up large St Andrew's crosses – but it's a bit like one of those trick pictures which look like one thing and end up being another. You have to concentrate to see the big crosses, but when you do it's not only obvious, but effective.

Sadly we won't see a real window treasure

• *Ladies with the hair plucked from their brows to make them more beautiful, others revelling in being pregnant, and a wedding day celebration. All included in this splendid painting of the marriage of Henry VI to Margaret of Anjou, which was once in a window in the south wall of the church.*

unless we go to the Bodleian Library. For a window in the south wall once had a mid-15th century painting which showed the marriage of Henry VI to Margaret of Anjou in 1445. Margaret was escorted to England by Robert Hungerford, whose brother Edmund, was Rector of Rollright at the time. There's a photograph of the painting on the table by the south wall however, which shows how the original was altered, for an anguished lady on the bottom left of the picture had her wringing hands removed and placed on the body of the man on the left who started off holding a falcon. The painting was made at the time the south aisle was built and shows the ladies with the foreheads plucked to show noble brows, and some are pregnant.

Although the painting has gone, the upper roundels of the window remain to show the Yorkist emblems of the white rose, and the falcon. It suggests some connection with Richard, Duke of York, who was later Richard III ('this glorious son of York'). The coronets there may also indicate a Ducal connection. It is thanks to Ald W.Fletcher of Yarnton that the painting survived for he rescued it, and it is thanks to Ann Darracott of the Maidenhead Civic Society that we know so much about it.

Most people think these are the only really old pieces of glass in the church, but a look at the top of the east window in the south aisle suggests some old fragments were used there as well.

Time now for our attempts to identify the church organ – in this case a plate reveals it was made by Porritt and Co, of the Midland Counties Organ Works at Loughborough and Leicester. It has the most marvellously decorated grained wood which is a far cry from the ubiquitous oak.

No good mentioning the organ without the bells, and once again we have the inscription 'William Bagley made mee' on the Third (1696) and the Fourth and Fifth (1695) which means they were made at the Chacombe bell foundry, as were so many other church bells in north Oxfordshire and further afield. The Second was made by Taylor, an Oxford Bellfounder in 1839, and the Treble by H.Bond and Sons of Burford. The other bell (1695) has the names of churchwardens, James Berry and Richard Beckett, inscribed on it.

Hidden away in the recess under the bell tower is a tablet commemorating a gift of £40 to the church for 'repewing' which guarantees 146 free seats for parishioners in perpetuity, and three large tombs set in the floor.

Echoes of pre-Christian times can be seen in the stone effigies of the Green Man and the Green Lady on the western window exterior on the south wall, and in some of the strange carvings on the south porch door.

Preaching cross, butter cross, or market cross? No matter what it was its remains are alongside the path to the church, and judging from the base it must have been quite a good size. Talking of markets, celebrations, and festivals,

• *Did the stonemason who carved the marvellous entrance to Enstone church pop down the road to Great Rollright and produce this equally fine carving at St Andrew's ?*

Great Rollright resembles Burton Dassett in that it has three broad steps leading up the sanctuary which in those far off days of church theatre must have provided a remarkable stage, not only for the enactment of morality plays, but for church ceremonial as well.

Certainly among the audience would have been the ancestors of the large brown mouse that was wandering around the children's corner in the church – perhaps in search of chocolate crumbs left by the youngsters, Poor as a church mouse? – Not this one – he was sleek, feisty, and had aspirations in size of becoming a rat! Don't be put off by that however, for he achieved a Formula One getaway from my sandal, and this church, described as 'a beautiful example of Gothic architecture' is well worth a visit.

• *The vibrant colours in the rood screen are echoed in this original section of the roof.*